RITUAL
BATHS

DEBORAH HANEKAMP

MORROW GIFT

An Imprint of WILLIAM MORROW

RITUAL
BATHS

))◐((

Be Your Own Healer

This book is dedicated to

HERMAN AND MUNAY

Thank you for the power of your LOVE.

Contents

Introduction

The wound is the place where the light enters you.

—RUMI

My first "ritual bath" was my baptism. I was eight years old. Most people at my church were not baptized until they were at least thirty, but I'd been determined from a young age to be as close as possible to the divine. I spent hours outside in the backwoods of northern Connecticut collecting crystals, talking to trees and animals, searching for and finding many different ways to pray. I was fascinated by John the Baptist and by the notion that someone's sins can be washed away. Even at eight years old, I intuited the importance of the baptismal ritual, and I wasn't about to wait twenty-two years to experience it for myself. Although my pastor tried to dissuade me, I could not be deterred and kept asking until he finally agreed to baptize me.

I remember standing at the altar looking out at the faces of my congregation. The murky blue, adult-size polyester baptism gown clung to my skin from my nervous sweat. I could smell the chlorine from the water and wondered what the temperature would be like. I quoted a Bible verse about the power of love. I remember how right it felt to stand up, in front of people, and talk about love. My pastor showed me a special way to hold my nose as I entered the water that felt incredibly sacred to me. I stepped into the large, cold bathtub. I dunked my head underwater. I did not exactly know what my sins were, but I felt them wash away. As I raised my head out of the water, I remember wishing that I could hold my breath for longer so that I could wash away more sins. I stepped out of the tub sopping wet and freezing, but happy to be born anew.

One month after my baptism, my pediatrician found a massive tumor during a routine checkup that was crushing my right ovary, fallopian tube, and appendix. I needed immediate surgery and spent the following month in the hospital in pain. Throughout this time, even with the knowledge that the tumor might destroy my chance of ever giving birth, I held on to the experience of my baptism and felt grateful to be alive. These are the events that gave me an early start on my mystical path. From then on, my life was consumed with trying to understand where my tumor came from and how I could heal myself so that one day I could become a mother.

When I was twelve, my family began to fall apart. My dad came home from work less and less and my mom began drinking more and more. We stopped going to church. Because of this, I began exploring new ways of connecting to spirit. I had always been able to see colors around people—it is as natural to me as feeling the sun on my face. One day, I mentioned this to some of the neighborhood kids; I realized from their reactions that this was highly unusual. I began turning to mystical books in search of answers. It was then that I realized that these colors I could see were called auras.

This led me to become fascinated with artists like William Blake, who painted the aura. I read his poetry along with that of other mystical poets including Rumi, Hafiz, and even Jim Morrison. My family situation continued to deteriorate, and I found myself on my own in the world when I turned seventeen. I knew I could either let the pain of my past become my future or I could surrender to the whispers of the mystical world, a world that made sense to me, one that could help me understand why I had these strong and difficult experiences at such an early age. I chose the latter path, and things were never the same again.

My second ritual bath changed my life. I was twenty-four and training to be a shaman in the Peruvian Amazon. As part of my instruction, I had to go on a *dieta*, a Peruvian shamanic initiation. On a *dieta*, you live in a small hut completely submerged in nature and open to the elements of the jungle. You fast to take on the energy of a specific plant assigned to you by a shaman to aid in your personal healing and balance. I was given *bubinzana* (a shrub from the *Mimosa*

family). *Bubinzana* grows by the riverside, and she is completely destroyed by the flooding river in the rainy season. But her roots are so strong that when the river quiets down again, she becomes a tiny sprout. Within one month, she is a full shrub. In three months, she is a fully blooming bush with bright pink, red, and purple flowers. For shamans, the medicine of this plant gives roots to those who experienced a tough early life. *Bubinzana* helps you rebuild yourself and bloom in spite of adversity.

Five days into my *dieta*, I found myself starting to resist. I felt beyond hungry and beyond bored with myself. All of the darkness I had been avoiding began flooding out of me, and I began to break down. Even after seven years of intense yoga practice, Zen training, Reiki courses, and endless study across the wide scope of healing arts, I had not even scratched the surface of the self-healing I needed to do. My visions became very dark, with bats and devils, and I felt completely terrified. For the first time, I couldn't find my light.

My teacher guided me to a nearby waterfall and commanded me to go under it. I let its water wash me, and when I felt a little better, I returned to him. He was standing over a big cauldron filled with plants, stirring and singing. He handed me clay and told me to cover myself in it and dry out in the sun. After an hour, he instructed me to go back under the waterfall. I did, and when I came back, he handed me honey to cover myself. As I spread the golden honey on my skin, I began to feel better and better. I returned to the waterfall once more. The entire time, my teacher kept stirring the contents of the cauldron and singing.

When I came out from under the waterfall for the third and last time, my teacher had me stand on top of a large quartz crystal rock. He began to dump the concoction he had been brewing over my head while singing a beautiful *icaro* (a shamanic medicine song) as he worked. In that moment, all of the darkness I had been living in washed away. I stepped out of the shadow that I had been carrying, not just for those intense few days, but since my childhood. I had finally found true light.

It was at that moment that I understood the healing powers of water and Ritual Bathing. I became enthralled with the different healing elements—the clay, the crystals, the herbs—that aided in my cleansing. The curious mystic in me began to explore all of the different spiritual tools I could bring into my daily bath to maintain my newly cleansed spirit. I began to create Ritual Baths uniquely crafted for auras, the cosmic calendar, and for what specifically needed healing, first for myself and then for others.

A Ritual Bath is no ordinary bath. It works with salt to cleanse and a smudging stick to bless, and it calls on the healing powers of various crystals, flowers, and herbs. Songs, mantras, prayers, and breathing exercises are all integrated to enhance the bath's healing energetic properties. These are the same Ritual Baths I now prescribe to clients after every Medicine Reading, my own shamanic healing ceremony, and to the larger population via social media. I believe that these Ritual Baths allow us to become our own healers, and combined with balanced lifestyle choices, can help us shine a light unto ourselves first, and create the opportunity for that light to radiate out into the world.

How to Use This Book

In a world where we are constantly immersed in loud external stimuli, it is easy to look outside of ourselves for the comfort, peace, and healing we need. But in order to truly heal and find our own way, we musn't look outward, but within. Each Ritual Bath I have created is designed to help you do just that.

After nearly twenty years of my accumulated experience in energetic healing and spiritual well-being, I have distilled everything I have learned into a new form of holistic therapy and healing—Medicine Readings. In a Medicine Reading, I help my clients realign and rebalance their energy, and ultimately, be their own healers. At the end of a Medicine Reading, I prescribe a Ritual Bath. These baths combine the ancient ritual of cleansing and meditating with the healing properties of everyday elements such as herbs, flowers, and crystals. These baths are not a magic potion to be used as a cure-all; however, the Ritual Baths along with the intention we put into them can bring about healing on a massive scale.

This book is a modern guide for becoming your own healer. Organized by aura color, it is designed to empower you to use your intuition to infuse your aura with that which will bring you balance. You do not need to see or know the color of your aura in order to choose which bath is right for you. You will simply know. Yes, you are intuitive! You are intuitive because you have feelings and feelings are a powerful guide to your wisdom, even though they may sometimes make you uncomfortable. That discomfort is imperative for your growth. You can use what you are feeling, what you are calling in, or what you are clearing out spiritually, emotionally, mentally, or physically from your life as your guide to choosing which bath to take and which color to infuse into your aura. We all have experienced how our emotions can influence our energy. Our feelings affect our auras in the same way, because our auras are simply our energy bodies.

THE MOON

Our emotions, the messages of our intuition, are represented by the element of water. Water, like how we feel, is always changing. Our bodies are made up of mostly water and, like the Earth, we are deeply influenced by the large gravitational field controlled by the sun and the moon. At the time of the new and full moon, our sun and moon affect the Earth, causing our ocean tides to rise to their highest. This force also pulls at the subtle bodies of water, causing moisture to rise in the earth, which encourages growth both in nature and inside of us, because we are a part of nature.

The new moon is the best time to plant the seeds of our intention or to call in energy. The full moon is a potent time to prune and ground ourselves to make room for new growth. I love lining my Ritual Baths up with the new or full moon. By following when they occur each month, you can do the same. Just like the moon, we are always changing, evolving, and growing. We are always rising and falling. We are always calling in or clearing out. For this reason, I have created a list of potent baths for what you are calling in or clearing out.

ASTROLOGY

While I believe in destiny, I also strongly believe that free will plays a huge part in who we are today and who we will become tomorrow. No matter the stars that you were born under, I feel that you have the power to choose what you will do with the life you have been given.

That being said, I see great value in knowing about your stars as a form of wisdom gaining and self-study. I see value in knowing what sign the moon is in, because it can guide us to grow in a certain way. When the moon is traveling through a specific sign, it can be a good time to work with the elements that the sign represents. For example, a Scorpio full moon (the sign that is the most comfortable with death) is the best time to prune the dead leaves on your plants so that new growth can occur. We can also learn from this process to release what is no longer needed in us. In each Ritual Bath, I've included the zodiac symbols that resemble the energy of the bath as a way to connect us here on Earth to the wonder and wisdom of our sky.

CHAKRAS

Do aura colors line up with chakra colors? In my ten years of teaching and training others to teach yoga, I have learned all about the chakra system and it makes a lot of sense to me. I see many places where aura colors and chakra colors align, and other places where they differ. If anything, I see them as a forced alignment. So, even though I find chakras and their colors fascinating, I've left their correlation to auras out of the book.

THE ELEMENTS

To me, working with the elements of Earth, Wind, Water, and Fire are the key ingredients to being your own healer. I believe in the power of these forces so much that I lead an annual retreat to teach women of all ages how to work with these elements both within and around them. Working with the elements helps us to not get too far out and travel off into the thirteenth dimension while we become more and more spiritually sensitive. You are on the planet Earth in the third dimension because you need to be here at this time. The Earth needs you here at this time. Yes, it is exciting when we feel our multidimensional selves, but we are experiencing that only so we can ground it down and use what we learn as medicine for ourselves and others. Working with the elements helps us to do this.

BATH INGREDIENTS

Some of the baths will be the actual aura color, while others will use plants and stones that are representative of that color but the bath water will remain clear. Some of the baths ask for more elaborate ingredients, while for others, all the ingredients you need can be found in your kitchen. I created an encyclopedia of ingredients (page 231) in order for you to understand the spiritual meaning behind the plants and stones for yourself. My hope is that you begin feeling confident enough to eventually make up some of your own baths intuitively.

Keep in mind that if you don't have all the ingredients, it's okay. Improvise or just leave that ingredient out. Your intention, the ritual, and the water are all you truly need for a transformative Ritual Bath. Improvisation is especially useful for crystals. I believe that our crystals find us. Sometimes on the beach, sometimes through a friend, and sometimes in a store. If I recommend a certain crystal but you feel called to use another that has been your ally, follow your intuition. You al-

Liquids

plants

smudging

salt

Candle

Crystals

ready have all the tools you need to be your own healer. Crystals, herbs, and even your bathtub are only external reminders of the consciousness you are putting into the work you do. My work is focused on empowering you to step into that place within you so that you may meet your own inner healer, your inner wisdom keeper. Ritual Baths are an amazing way to understand how much you possess the power to heal yourself. Listen to your inner guide—the love within you—and improvise, mix, match, and combine baths.

A go-to pantry list of items that I recommend having on hand for Ritual Bathing:

- A candle
- A cinnamon stick for smudging yourself
- Salt for your bath
- Fresh or dried rosemary for your bath
- Found feather

If you have found a feather in nature, you can use it to waft the smoke around your body. I encourage you to use only feathers that you have found or that a friend has found and given to you, as when you buy feathers (or any animal material for that matter) you can't be sure exactly how the feather ended up in the store. Some practices for gathering feathers and other animal material are cruel, and if a healing tool is received through cruelty or exploitation of any kind, then it is no longer healing. It's simply adding to the suffering that greed causes in our human hearts. When you find a feather in nature, it is the universe's way of giving you a gift and the feather is a spiritual tool that you are meant to use. It's us if to say that you have completed a journey or spiritual sojourn of some kind and are now ready to level up in some way. Accept this gift and leave something behind in gratitude. You can offer tobacco, sage, or just your love. It is fun to feed the creative spirit and make a wand for yourself from the feathers you have found, even if it takes a few years to create. It is powerful to combine differ-

ent herbs together during your smudging practice, the practice of burning dried plants around the body or around a room to cleanse the auric field.

A selenite wand is the main crystal used to cleanse the aura. Selenite is actually a salt, so please limit it to outside-of-the-bath practices only. You also may want to wrap one end of your selenite wand in some kind of fabric. This is a very delicate stone, so make sure you keep it in a special place.

The temperature of the water you bathe in is up to you.

YOUR OWN EXPERIENCE

A very important note when using this book is to understand that you do not need to believe in any particular thing in order to feel the calm strength of the baths. Yes, I talk of angels, guides, and past lives, but this is based only on my experience. If you experience and see things differently, that is wonderful. Take what works for you and leave the rest behind. I want you to feel powerful, not obedient. Truthfully, although I am mystical, I am also quite the skeptic when it comes to a lot of what is out there in the spiritual wellness space. I got into this world at a very young age and have seen a lot of people giving their power away to gurus sitting on pedestals and treating everyone who follows them like they are beneath them. I've met a lot of people working as healers who were so ungrounded and spaced out that they couldn't keep a relationship, home, or schedule, or pay their taxes. I've even seen people become addicted to plant medicine, to healers, and to shamans. In those identifying as spiritual not religious, I've seen a lot of dogma, restriction, and piety. When I started out on this path I was a young, good-looking kid, and I can't count how many dirty old men under the guise of yoga teachers, meditation teachers, massage therapists, shamans, and healers were total creeps to me. They were twice my age and would use their authority to make

up spiritual reasons as to why I should sleep with them (which fortunately I was rebellious enough to see through).

So when someone tells me that they are a healer, I question what they actually mean by that. I run everything I read, see, and hear through my own truth processing system—my intuition. I ask that as you use this book, you do the same. I would never want you to do something just because I say you should. I want you to do what feels right for you. Please take everything written here as suggestion and opinion. When someone comes for a Medicine Reading or on one of my retreats and asks me what their dream or some other symbol they have seen means, I turn the question back to them: "What does it mean to you?" My giving you all the answers is so much less empowering than you figuring them out for yourself. This is the way you truly learn. My beloved, your truth is in you. Not I nor anyone else can tell you where you should go or what you should do because they do not have your magic.

Then I said, "You asked me if I thought your visions were true.

I would say that they were if they made you become more human,

more kind to every creature and plant that you know."

—HAFIZ

I AM CALLING IN

RED
Getting Grounded Bath
Ancestors Bath

Location and Home Bath
Awareness = Protection Bath

Strength Bath

ORANGE
For All My Relationships Bath

Money Bath

Fertility Bath

YELLOW
Ally Bath
Healthy Boundaries Bath

Warrior Bath
Find My Purpose Bath

Gut Bath
Confidence Bath

GREEN
Awareness Wolf Bath
Empath Bath

Hope Bath
I Am Nature Bath

Be My Own Healer Bath
Love of My Life Bath

BLUE
Spirit Guides Bath
Spirit Babies Bath

*Communication and
Connection Bath*

Trust Bath

INDIGO
Sacred Rebel Bath
Deep Listening Bath

Intuition Bath
We Are All Connected Bath

Truth Bath

VIOLET
Dream Medicine Bath

New Moon Bath

Mercury Direct Bath

ACCENT COLORS

OPALESCENT
Past Lives Bath

MAGENTA
New Love Bath

I AM CLEARING OUT

RED

Releasing Attachment Bath   *Birth Bath*

ORANGE

Creativity Bath   *Forgiveness, Celebration,*
Sexual Healing Bath   *Happiness Bath*

YELLOW

Know Thyself/New Beginnings   *Be Seen Bath*
Bath   *Addiction Healing Bath*

GREEN

Awareness Wolf Bath   *Mercury Retrograde*
Forgiveness Bath

BLUE

Integrity Bath   *Open Up Bath*   *Judgment Release Bath*

INDIGO

Unwounded Bath

VIOLET

Grief Bath   *Full Moon Bath*   *Dream Medicine Bath*
Unity Bath   *Spirit Cleansing Bath*

ACCENT COLORS

SILVER   **GOLD**   **OPALESCENT**   **MAGENTA**
De-Armor Yourself Bath   *Mandala Ritual Bath*   *Past Lives Bath*   *New Love Bath*

SHADOW AND LIGHT

To be our own healers, we must be balanced. Our light and shadow are neither good or bad.

Our shadow is the dark and dusty corner of our self that we prefer to keep hidden. It can be our pasts, the habits and patterns we have that no longer serve us, and our ancestral wounds. If we integrate and assimilate our shadow rather than try to reject it, we can gain wisdom and grow. It may be hard for us to be honest with ourselves about these things, but neglecting our shadow can truly make us feel ungrounded and lost. Think about plants. Most of them need to have roots down in the nutrient rich darkness of the earth in order to reach bravely toward the light. We are not so different.

Our light is the power of love within us. When we experience some of it, we want more of it because it feels so good. It's our kindness and gentleness that keep us curious, open, and accepting of the newness even in our old age. In every thought we have and action we take, we are presented with a choice. One of those decisions will keep us in a shadowy loop, because we may have not yet learned the necessary lesson it was teaching. This decision gives us another chance to learn that lesson. The other choice presents us with a guiding light toward more love, new experiences, and new lessons to learn.

What I've noticed in the past two decades on this spiritual path is that we are never done working on ourselves. We are never done growing. We can always become more loving. Love, kindness, and receptivity are, to me, the markings of a truly spiritual human. I don't look at what you do for work, what you wear, what you believe in, what you eat or drink, what you do for fun. I look at whether you are loving to yourself and others and whether you take the many opportunities you have in any given day to express kindness. Then I see a true master, a true healer, in you because the true master, the true healer, is love.

Aura Cleansing and Blessing

THE AURA DEMYSTIFIED

You know that feeling when you are about to turn a corner and somehow you feel that you'll bump into someone around the bend if you don't move? Or when you feel someone staring at you without even seeing them? When someone walks into an already occupied room and the mood of the original group changes? All of this is "sensing energy." We are so much more than flesh, bones, and mind. We are infinitely connected to the world around us. Just as we each have a physical body, we also have an energetic body, or an aura.

The concept of auras appears in some of our earliest cultures. The word *aura* originates from the ancient Greek language, meaning "breath, wind, or breeze." Yogis refer to it as the *pranamaya kosha*. In Sanskrit, the word *prana* is used to describe both breath and energy. In China, the aura is referred to as *chi*, and in Japan, *ki*. Early Christian and Egyptian paintings depict halos around the heads of figures, and Hildegard von Bingen, a first-century healer, nun, and prophetess, spoke of seeing light around people.

As humankind shifted from a matriarchal society to a patriarchal society, the aura and its recording were forgotten in the West. Aside from a brief revival by the Theosophical Society around 1910, belief in auras was limited until the New Age movement of the 1970s. Through the years, skeptics have devised countless tests trying to trip up those who claim they can see auras, to "prove" that the human energy field doesn't exist. Truth be told, if I were to take some of these tests, I would probably fail to see the aura too. Trying to prove whether or not auras are real would be as difficult as trying to prove what happens after we die or how we fall in love—it is among the great mysteries in life and cannot be completely logically defined.

I first realized that not everyone could see auras when I was twelve years old. There I was, fully loaded with freckles, a funny haircut, and multicolored elastic bands on my braces, talking to my friends about the shapes and colors around people and what they meant. My friends looked at me like I was crazy, and I realized that they couldn't see what I saw. The awkwardness and embarrassment of that experience led me, for a long time, to discuss auras only with those closest to me. As I've aged, I've learned to release this fear and to share my unique gifts.

I've also learned to articulate what I see in people's auras to help them uncover possible obstacles or hidden talents and gifts in their own lives, so that they may live in balance, authenticity, and joy. This offering, followed by a multisensory shamanic ceremony, is called a Medicine Reading; it's the modality I invented after fifteen years on my own powerful spiritual journey.

Sometimes people who cannot see auras want to learn how to see them. My answer is that we are all able to sense energy one way or another. Whether we do so through scent, sight, sound, feeling, or even taste is dependent on our individual gifts. To nurture and cultivate your own gifts, here are a few things that can help put you in a more receptive state of mind:

1. Get enough sleep.
2. Spend less time looking at a screen and more time looking at nature.
3. Meditate consistently.
4. Practice *trataka*, a candle meditation that yogis practice to cleanse the eyes.
5. Eat healthfully and avoid toxins.
6. Spend time alone.

I am still not sure if you can *learn* how to see auras, but after having cultivated a receptive state of mind, here's how you can try. Once you are ready, have a friend stand in front of a white wall in a well-lit room. Stand facing them, close your

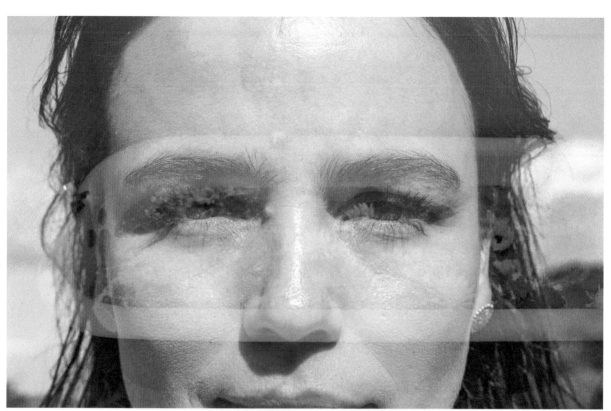

eyes, and take three deep breaths. Open your eyes and look at them, letting your vision blur a little bit. Be patient and the aura may reveal itself.

The first two questions I'm often asked are "What color is my aura?" and "What does that mean?" Most people have different colors in their auras and in varying amounts. Different colors and shapes in different places within the aura signify different things. Our moods can also shift the colors of our auras. For example, when someone is feeling very confident and open they will have a large, bright, multicolored aura. Someone who is feeling more withdrawn can have an almost single-colored aura that hugs closely to the body.

These color combinations make deciphering and properly translating auras a complex craft that requires spending a good amount of time speaking with and learning about each person. Ultimately, reading auras is like learning to speak an esoteric language with no one to teach you and no text to refer to. To decode this language is quite complicated, but for fun I will share with you the tip of the iceberg of what some of these colors mean to me:

What color is my aura?

RED	Grounded, passionate, materialistic, business interactions, family oriented, strong
ORANGE	Creative, receptive, pregnant, ability to wake dreams into reality, needs being met
YELLOW	Joy, health, new beginnings, positive thoughts, awareness, protected, addiction
GREEN	A natural healer, compassionate, empathy, love, parenting, very connected to the earth
BLUE	Balance and deep need for balance to be maintained, organized, teacher, momentous life event on the horizon
INDIGO	Game changer, difficult early life, here to help, strong sense of purpose, depression if not on path, sacred rebel
VIOLET	Dreamer, spiritually aware, shyness, protective, leader

WHY WOULD THE AURA NEED TO BE
CLEANSED AND BLESSED?

Just as our physical bodies need cleansing, our energy bodies need cleansing too. Maybe we have had an intense day at work, have just ridden a packed subway with a crowd of other people and feel overwhelmed, or just feel inexplicably "heavy." Whatever the case, feeling this way means it is a good time to cleanse the aura.

Before prescribing a Ritual Bath, I like to offer a pre-cleansing of the auric field as a method of preparation and honoring the healing you are about to give yourself. Now that you have an understanding of how you may be able to begin to see auras and what each color aura can mean, you will sense a deeper connection to the energy around you. In the next chapters, I will further reveal how auras are relevant to Ritual Baths and why we might need to cleanse our auras with baths in order to protect ourselves. In the encyclopedia of ingredients at the end of the book, I list some herbs that help cleanse the aura. It would be beneficial to get to know these herbs as preface for the Ritual Bath recipes that are the heart of the book.

Liquids · salt · smudging · powders · plants

Wheel of the year

Elemental Correspondences

The human body is made up of 60 percent water. The water in our bodies and the waters of the Earth move and change with the gravitational pull of the moon. When the moon is new or full, it creates a bulge in the ocean, causing stronger tides and possible storms. Our brains are also made up mostly of water. Could this be why emotions run high on new and full moons? Since the element of water is the connection to our emotional bodies, on new moons, full moons, supermoons, and lunar and solar eclipses, our emotions can be all over the place.

On a new moon, we may find ourselves crying all day as we cleanse the old habits and patterns that no longer serve us. Or we may find that we feel aggressive, even frustrated, on a full moon, as she shines a bright light on us revealing what needs to be healed.

The moon and the sweet, soft darkness of the night sky surrounding her naturally encourage us to go into a more reflective state. The more we succumb to this natural urge, the more balanced and connected we feel. Simple acts like journaling on a new moon, making medicine on a full moon, or cleaning out our rooms on a waning gibbous moon help us to connect with the natural flow of the moon and therefore with the flow of the water in our bodies.

Since the dawn of agriculture, farmers have known to plant seeds on a new moon, harvest on a full, prune on a waxing gibbous, and trim and fertilize on a waning gibbous. Before we began zoning out with technology at night, our ancestors were tapping into the night sky and our sister the moon, putting the responsibility of their lives in her wise and loving hands. Although we no longer need to be out farming all day in order to survive, we can still connect to the moon to find balance in the water of our bodies and our emotions. For women within bleeding ages, a good sign that you are in alignment with the moon and her ever changing presence is getting your "moon cycle," or bleed, with the new moon or full moon. Bleeding with the new moon signifies that you are trying to be open and receptive; bleeding with the full moon means that you are trying to shine and to allow yourself to be seen.

Through submerging yourself in water and bathing with the moon phases, you set an intention of connection to our bright sister, the moon. She is such a powerful representation of our divine feminine wisdom. Ever present yet ever changing. Reflecting the sun's own light back to him. Sister moon encourages us to open our voices and sing to her—owl, wolf, cricket, and human alike—reminding us through the unity of our songs how connected we all are and how, just like her, we are born, we grow, we fade, and we go.

Moons

phases

WANING MOON ENERGY

This is a time of release and surrender. What are you hanging on to that no longer serves you? Clear out clutter in your home, mind, and heart. Take baths focused on energy cleansing. Offer crystals or trimmed plants to the Earth.

NEW MOON ENERGY

As you're feeling more cleared out, what are the last things or patterns that you can let go of? Cut your hair and offer it to the Earth to release the old energy that was held there. Cry if you need to and then let yourself rest. All that release and surrender is exhausting! When you are ready, take time to plant new seeds, literally or figuratively. Set your intentions through journaling, maybe even lighting a candle and focusing your intention into the flame. Perhaps send your focus into a quartz crystal and plant that crystal in the earth to ground your intention, to be dug up again on the full moon to hold and receive revelations about that intention. This is a great time for baths by candlelight that involve singing.

WAXING MOON ENERGY

Now is the time to nourish the seeds of intention that you planted. What can you actively do to help that intention to grow? Sometimes it is enough to simply plant a seed and let time and nature take care of it. But often if we really want something to grow, we have to actively nourish it. It is the same with our intentions. For example, if you set an intention on the new moon to find work you love, now is the time to put in applications, network, and knock on doors. Working with waxing moon energy through ritual can be done through journaling, taking reflective evening walks, and taking baths that have activating ingredients in them like cinnamon, basil, and amethyst crystals.

FULL MOON ENERGY

Work hard, play hard. You've done your best to nourish your intentions. Now is the time to celebrate your growth in the direction of your intention. Make medicine, sing, dance, howl, socialize, and share. The full moon is all about revelations. What is being shown to you today? Your light and shadow are very visible at this time. See it all. Acknowledge and celebrate it! Without our shadow, how can we obtain the wisdom needed to reach toward our light? Take baths that make you feel beautiful. Use flowers that are in full bloom like our sister, the moon.

The Elements

air

fire

THE ELEMENTS—*Wind, Fire, Water, and Earth—are just as much around us as within us. Wind is our breath, our communication, our truth. Fire is our wild spirit, our purity, our passion, our clarity, and our discernment. Water is our blood, our connection to all that is, our emotions, our intuition. Earth is our body, our abundance, our growth, our guide (your wise body is always guiding you toward what you need). When we work with the elements of nature, we are being our own healers, because we are a part of nature. Even if we were never taught about the changing tides, we can feel our connection to the elements. Stand outside on a windy day and let your hair down, let your arms rise up. Can you not feel the wind cleansing your spirit? The elements speak to us even if we have never consciously connected with them.*

When we do connect with them, we find that the elements within and around us have been waiting for us to begin working with them. When you bring the elements into your Ritual Baths, you are helping to ground the powerful work you are doing. You can use a talisman to represent each element. For example: a found feather or a smudge for Wind; a candle for Fire; the water of your bath for Water; and crystals or plants for Earth. The elements also each link up with specific cardinal directions.

water

earth

Cardinal Directions

EAST, SOUTH, WEST, NORTH

In my travels to Peru, I learned about the importance of sending a blessing to and calling in the directions. I then noticed that calling in the directions is a pre- and post-ceremonial practice in ancient traditions worldwide. When we invoke the direction before a Ritual Bath, the experience becomes that much more ceremonious for us.

To invoke a direction, use a compass to see where each direction is. You can place your sacred corresponding talisman in each direction. Begin with East, because it is the direction of the new, then South, West, and North. Stand straight and tall with your palms facing that direction and call in the direction in whichever way you usually pray. I created a song that I like to sing to invoke the directions. It goes:

Clean my energy, help me say what I mean
Clean my energy Sacred Wind
Sacred Wind in the East
I call on your Grace
I call on your Grace
I call on your Grace, Sacred Wind in the East

Purify me spiritually, help me see reality
Purify me spiritually Sacred Fire

Sacred Fire in the South
Sacred Fire in the South
I call on your Grace
I call on your Grace
I call on your Grace
Sacred Fire in the South

Hold me lovingly, teach me receptivity
Hold me lovingly Sacred Water
Sacred Water in the West
Sacred Water
Sacred Water in the West
I call on your Grace
I call on your Grace
I call on your Grace
Sacred Water in the West

Watch over me, nourish my possibilities
Guide me Sacred Earth
Sacred Earth in the North
I call on your Grace
I call on your Grace
I call on your Grace
Sacred Earth in the North

Cardinal directions will be included in each bath to help you understand the ancientness of the energy you are working with. You can page through this book and try a bath that aligns you with a direction you feel called to. By using the book this way, you might discover and find the ways you are seeking direction.

Signs

Aquarius

pisces

aries

Taurus

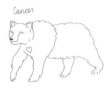
Cancer

Leo

Virgo

Libra

scorpio

Sagittarius

Capricorn

The energy of the moon and sun can be altered by the sign they fall under. Individually and collectively, our feelings can be altered by the astrological signs they fall under because we are so very guided by the sun and moon. As another tool to guide you toward what baths to take, I've added astrological symbols to each aura color and also beside each bath. It can feel very aligning for you to take a certain bath when the moon, sun, or planets that speak to you are in a specific sign or if the sign lines up with the sun, moon or rising sign you were born under. Here are descriptions of what each sign symbolizes:

Aquarius:	New visions
Pisces:	Curiosity
Aries:	Intelligence
Taurus:	Steady
Gemini:	Playful
Cancer:	Dreamer
Leo:	Purity
Virgo:	Grounded
Libra:	Balance driven
Scorpio:	Sacred rebel
Sagittarius:	Radiance
Capricorn:	Leader

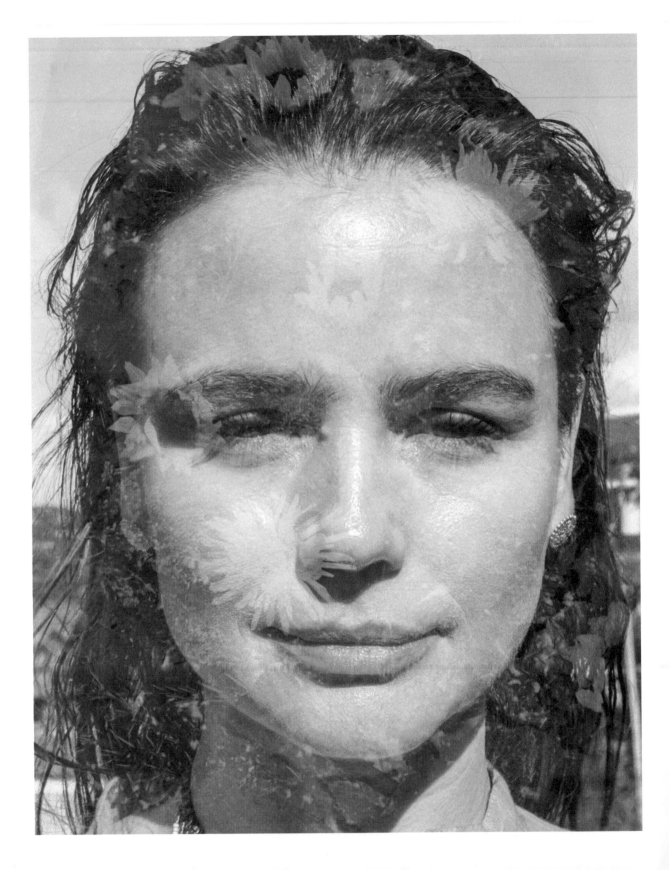

Seasons

The seasons can also have a strong effect on our well-being. I will use symbols of the seasons throughout the book as another tool to guide you to the bath that is right for you on a given day. It doesn't need to be spring outside for you to want to take a spring bath. It just means you are having a moment when you want to call in or clear out the energy of spring within you.

Spring: New beginnings, hope, grief

Summer: Abundance, love, anger

Fall: Cleansing, creativity, anxiety

Winter: Silence, reflection, rest, depression

Tea Pairings

With each bath, I have suggested a tea that would be lovely to sip as you soak. To make your tea, simply place the suggested herbs (fresh or dried) into a teapot or tea bag. Place a clean rose quartz crystal in your teapot. If you feel called to, it can be powerful to sing into your tea before you drink it. Just like with everything in this book, use what you have and don't worry about being too precise! Your intention is what really matters.

Getting Started

In my training in Amazonian Shamanism, I was taught that one way to measure a shaman's skill is by assessing their ability to properly open and close a ceremony. If you think about it, some of the most important things in life follow this pattern. For example, how you interview for a job determines the position you will get at that company, and the way in which you choose to exit a job determines whether you'll get a recommendation from your former employer. The way we start relationships can determine the level of trust that we have in our partners, and the way we end that relationship can predict the amount of time it will take us to heal before we begin again. If you are a painter and you take time to properly set up your workstation, placing all the paints and oils you will need in front of you, it makes the creative process of painting that much more supported. When you are finished, you wash your brushes and cleanse your palette, signifying that the process is done.

When we consciously begin and close experiences, everything in life can become a ceremony. I've applied this method to all of my spiritual practices and have experienced that as I open a ceremony, there is a feeling of joy and excitement about what is to come. As I close a ceremony, there is a feeling of gratitude and understanding, no matter how big or small the ceremony.

A Ritual Bath can have a beautiful and elaborate opening and closing. You can sprinkle fresh and dried flowers on the surface of the water, surround yourself with lit candles, immerse yourself in the beauty of the Earth's love by placing crystals all around you and in your water. Closing it involves some cleanup, but even this is part of the ceremony and should not be rushed.

Below I will give you proper opening and closing techniques for both an elaborate and a simple Ritual Bath. As we go through the book, I will note when certain herbs or crystals would be "the dream" to have in your bath but they might be more difficult to find.

ELABORATE RITUAL BATH

OPENING

- Choose your Ritual Bath. Gather your supplies. Whenever possible, use beautiful seasonal herbs, organic flowers, and raw honey.
- The night before your bath, place the herbs from the ingredients into a pot. Bring it to a simmer and then take it off the heat. Let it sit overnight to create an infusion. This tea will later be poured into your bath.
- Before your bath, clean your bathroom and tub. Place candles around to make the space feel grounded and inviting.
- When you are ready to bathe, fill the bath and carefully place the crystals into the tub in order to let them infuse the water for as long as possible.
- Add the remaining ingredients to your tub.
- Follow the ritual from there.

CLOSING

- Step out of the tub and dry yourself off with nurturing care.
- Blow out your candles with gratitude, releasing your intention into the universe.
- Remove the flowers and herbs from the tub. Set them aside in a bowl to bring as an offering to a nearby tree.
- Collect as much of your bath water as you can to give as an offering to the Earth. (I currently live in New York City, and after each bath, I wash the sidewalks in front of my house to bless and protect my home.)
- Place the crystals on a windowsill to charge in the moonlight and sunlight.
- Lovingly clean out your tub.

SIMPLE RITUAL BATH

OPENING

- Light a candle in your bathroom. Fill the bathtub with water.
- Create a tub tea by putting pinches of herbs in a copper tea strainer or muslin bag and placing it directly in your tub.
- Place a crystal in the tub.
- If flowers are listed in the ingredients, put the petals of one flower on the surface of the water.
- Proceed with your Ritual Bath.

CLOSING

- Offer herbs and petals from the bath to a tree whenever you have time.

NOTE: As a working mom, I completely understand feeling like you are in a race against time. Even if you cannot open and close the Ritual Bath as above, simply lighting and then blowing out a candle will symbolically open and close the ceremony and give you a more complete feeling in your Ritual Bath.

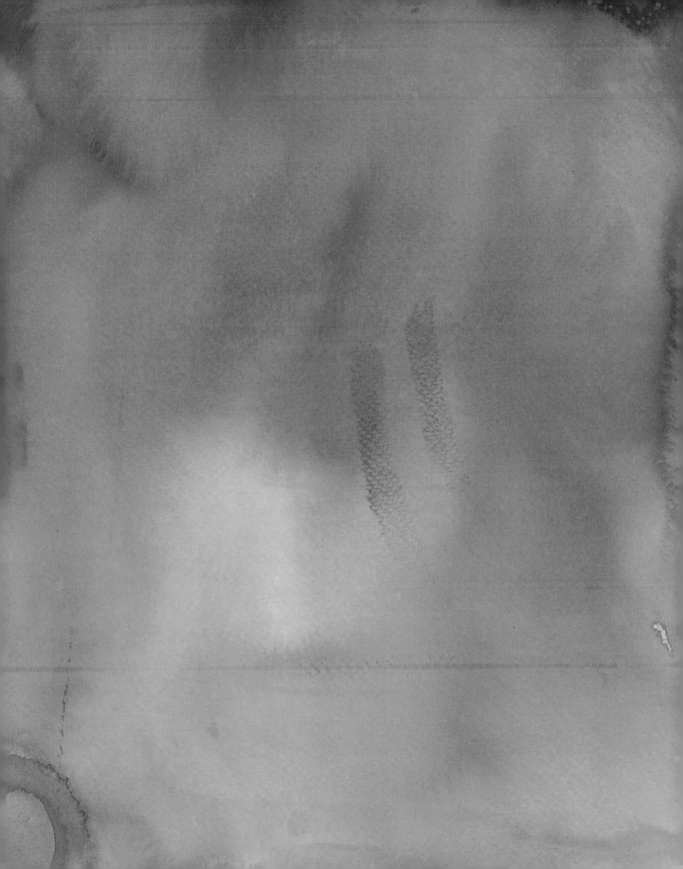

I

Red

Red is the color to call into your aura when you are having a hard time getting grounded and organized. It's a good color to help you see your point of view or make necessary changes in your life. When you are having a difficult time finishing things, getting ready to begin something new, or trying to find your dream home, red will help you bring into existence all that is meant for you.

THE LIGHT

Red people are get-it-done people. They are the ones you want by your side when you are giving birth, moving, or starting a new business. Reds excel at all things birth, life, and family. They are great at getting to the heart of a matter to create more clarity. Reds can visit a place once, come back ten years later, and still know their way around. Connected to their homes and families, they are generally very loyal. They take very good care of their physical bodies and material belongings. Grounded to the earth, they almost never feel lost.

THE SHADOW

Because Reds are so powerful, if they are not careful, they can disempower others. Reds are the most apt to intolerance, indifference, stubbornness, and judgment. They can be very fixed and rigid, and they find it difficult to make necessary moves in life or tolerate points of view that are different from their own. Reds will often stay in a relationship, job, or home long past its due date because they are so afraid of change. If you are not into following maps and sticking to schedules, Reds are not the best people to travel with. Definitely don't expect any go-with-the-flow spontaneity here. Reds want to stick to the schedule and get to where they are going as quickly as possible. Prone to being materialistic, Reds can put too much attention into what they own, allowing it to define them, and they can fall into the trap of comparison.

RED BATHS

GETTING GROUNDED BATH

ANCESTORS BATH

RELEASING ATTACHMENTS BATH

LOCATION AND HOME BATH

AWARENESS = PROTECTION BATH

BIRTH BATH

STRENGTH BATH

Getting Grounded Bath

NORTH, EARTH, VIRGO, WINTER
TEA PAIRING: KAVA TEA

The eye is naturally drawn to Red's power. People usually have a strong feeling about the color itself. I believe that this has something to do with the fact that if we let it, Red will remind and even return us to the truth of who we are and where we come from. If you are trying to escape yourself and your past, you may have an adverse reaction to red. But escaping ourselves and not owning where we come from will almost always leave us feeling ungrounded and scattered. This bath is designed to give you a moment of quiet and calm so that you can connect to the home you carry within you, wherever you may be.

Ingredients

1 cup Epsom salt
A pot of green or black tea
A pot of kava tea
2 red potatoes, sliced
1 purple potato, sliced

2 cups red rose petals, fresh or dried
10 drops of lavender and 3 drops of vetiver
    essential oils
Smoky quartz crystal

For a clarifying and brightening face mask while you are in the bath, mash the white part of one of the red potatoes, mix it with water, apply it to your skin, and leave it on for thirty minutes.

Ritual

- Place all the ingredients in the bath at a temperature of your choosing.
- Light some candles and turn off any overhead or artificial lights.
- Turn off all music/ambient noise, and let yourself get very quiet.
- Create a smudge using a cinnamon stick by putting it in a nonflammable tray of some kind and igniting it. Waft the smoke around your body using a feather you have found.
- Wave the smoking cinnamon stick over your bath and ask the water to help you come into the moment. Ask the water to help you to come home to yourself.
- Step into the bath and dunk your head underwater.
- Apply the potato face mask.
- Place the smoky quartz on your heart.
- Focus on all the sensations you are experiencing: the water on your skin, the smell of the essential oils, the beauty of the rose petals and potato slices floating around in the tub. When your mind drags you back to *I should* or *I have to*, bring your awareness back to the sensations you are experiencing. Eventually you will find yourself very present, very grounded, and simply soaking in the magic you've created.

Ancestors Bath

NORTH, EARTH, CAPRICORN, WINTER
TEA PAIRING: WHITE PINE AND ROSEWOOD TEA

One day in a Medicine Reading Ceremony, I asked the women in the room to claim themselves in the space and call in one of their spirit guides. The woman sitting to my right stated her name and then called in the spirit of her paternal grandmother. During the ceremony, I saw this very beautiful bright blue grandmother with glowing threads in her hands. I almost didn't have to do any healing work at all on the woman because she was receiving healing from the spirit of her grandmother. After the ceremony, I opened up the space for anyone who wanted to share a bit about their experience or ask any questions. The woman shared that she had been having massive pain in her lower back and pelvis for a while and during the ceremony, it had felt as if that pain had been removed and replaced with a bright glowing golden light. This is very interesting to me, because the lower back is the place where we carry our ancestral stories.

Even if we are not connected to or do not know about our human ancestors, our ancestors are all around us. They are in the tall trees, the ever-receptive water, the wise crystals and minerals, Grandmother Earth herself. All of these elements were here long before we came and most will remain after we leave. When we are in need of wisdom or when we are trying to remember, we can turn to the ever available energy of nature. This bath specifically helps connect us to the source of our inner ancestors, our internal knowing, our instincts, and our wisdom.

Ingredients

1 cup pink Himalayan sea salt

Infusion: 1 cup white pine needles, ½ cup rosemary (sprigs or dried), ½ cup mugwort, and ¾ cup elderberries. Infuse in 8 cups almost-boiling water and let steep for 24 hours.

3 cups fresh or dried red rose petals

3 drops of rosewood, 5 drops of cedarwood, and 8 drops of rosemary essential oils mixed into 1 cup raw local honey

Clear quartz crystal

Any crystals or stones you've found out in nature

Ritual

- Place all the ingredients in the bath at a temperature of your choosing.
- Light a candle with the intention of receiving ancestral wisdom.
- Create a smudge using dried cedar leaves, whole cloves, and broken cinnamon sticks by putting them in a nonflammable tray of some kind and igniting them. Waft the smoke around your body using a feather you have found.
- Step into the bath and dunk your head underwater.
- Coming up to a resting position, begin to take deep breaths, inhaling to a count of four and exhaling to a count of six.
- Place your hands on the surface of the water, connect to the energy of the water, and receive its wisdom.
- Hold the crystals or stones in your hands, place them on your feet, heart, belly, and forehead. Connect to the energy of the crystals or stones and receive their wisdom.
- Smell and feel the energy of the plants in your bath, receive their wisdom.
- Sit and soak in the medicine you've created.

Releasing Attachments Bath

SOUTH, FIRE, SAGITTARIUS, AUTUMN
TEA PAIRING: SHATAVARI AND CINNAMON LATTE

In the shadow energy of Red, we can hold ourselves back by being unwilling to let go of things that no longer serve us. Outdated trauma, habits, patterns, material belongings, homes, occupations, and even relationships that have long since served their purposes are kept around because we are afraid of change. I don't know that we ever truly let things go, but I do think that we can take the things that we've experienced and, rather than replay them over and over again, clear them of the labels "this was good" or "that was bad." From there we can simply distill the wisdom that each experience had to offer us. We can then integrate this wisdom by turning it into the medicine we need, helping ourselves to be free of the pattern. When the lesson has been learned, we can move forward and onward in our lives. Take this bath when you know that it is time for you to release something but are having trouble keeping the wisdom you need to move on.

Ingredients

A pinch of shatavari

A pinch of rosemary

A pinch of thyme

A pinch of green tea

A pinch of cardamom pods

3 red apples, sliced

3 cups apple juice

5 cinnamon sticks

2 cups red and white rose petals

Smoky quartz, amethyst, and citrine crystals

3 drops of cardamom and 10 drops of rose absolute essential oils

Ritual

- Place all the ingredients in the bath at a temperature of your choosing.
- Light a candle.
- Create a smudge using white sage by putting it in a nonflammable tray of some kind and igniting it. Waft the smoke around your body using a feather you have found.
- Step into the bath and dunk your head underwater.
- Place the crystals by your feet.

- Bring your awareness to your breath. Inhale through the nose to a count of four, then exhale through the nose to a count of eight.
- On each exhale, let yourself release from your body, mind, and spirit that which you know you must let go.
- Ask the water of the bath to help you embrace the changes that must come and to release attachment.
- Sit and soak in the medicine you've created.

Location and Home Bath

WATER, WEST, TAURUS, AUTUMN
TEA PAIRING: TULSI (COMMONLY CALLED HOLY BASIL) CHAI TEA

Red is a powerful color to call into your aura when you are trying to find your dream home or are wondering where you should live. We have to be a bit careful with the idea of being too specific when it comes to manifestation. I think, instead, we should keep our hearts and minds open to the fact that the universe may have something amazing in store for us if we allow ourselves be surprised.

For some of us, it can be really hard to ground and find a home. Some of us are always moving, always traveling. It's who we have become and how we identify. Then something in life shifts. We find a great job that requires us to be in a specific location or we have children who need to go to school. It is possible to seek a home with a flowing energy, so that we don't start to feel trapped in the more settled life we now require. There are some of us (my family included) who have a difficult time deciding where to ground. It's an interesting problem when you feel that you can be happy anywhere and nowhere all at the same time. Until it becomes very clear where you should be, the most powerful thing to do is simple: Stay where you are. This bath can help you to be open to finding the home that is the best medicine for you. Who knows? It may be the one you are already in.

Ingredients

3 cups pink Himalayan sea salt

A pot of chai tea

4 cups cranberry juice

3 cups oat milk

1 tablespoon honey

Red rose petals

10 drops each of rose absolute and vetiver
   essential oils

All of your non-water-soluble crystals

Ritual

- Place all the ingredients in the bath at a temperature of your choosing.
- Take a moment before you begin to make a playlist of all the songs that feel like home to you. Ideally these would be songs that would compel you to sing along

while you are in your bath, as well as ones that are just so very comforting to you to hear. When you are done creating your playlist, play it.

- Light candles and turn off any overhead lights.
- Create a smudge using a cinnamon stick by putting it in a nonflammable tray of some kind and igniting it. Waft the smoke around your body using a feather you have found.
- Step into the bath and dunk your head underwater.
- Place crystals on your body wherever you are able to. I suggest including your forehead and your hands.
- Close your eyes and ask the water to guide you. Ask the water to give signs either while you are in the bath or after you get out that will help you to clearly see how to create a healthy and happy living experience for yourself.

Awareness = Protection Bath

FIRE, SOUTH, LEO, SUMMER
TEA PAIRING: ROSE HIP, HIBISCUS, AND PASSION FRUIT TEA

Awareness = protection.

Red is a color that gets us to immediately pay attention. Call the color of red into your aura when you know you need to focus and pay attention.

When we are calling in protection, what we are truly calling in is the presence and power of love. Accidents don't usually happen when we are paying attention. They happen only when we are distracted. The more distracted we are, the less protected we are. This is true in our daily lives, as well as in our auric fields. When someone is distracted and ungrounded, their aura appears porous to me. When someone is focused and knows themselves, their aura is tight and very well protected.

One thing that can bring us awareness almost immediately is pain. Pain is something that the universe sends us when we are distracted and need to start paying attention right away. If you are bumping your head or stubbing your toes a lot, it is a sign that it is time for you to start paying attention. Awareness = protection.

The power of love is the most powerful form of protection.

Think of rose, so open, receptive, and symbolic of love, yet she is covered in thorns of awareness. You have to pay attention to how you harvest her, and if you approach her unaware you will get pricked. When you feel you need protection, focus on what you love the most in this world. This will tighten up your aura and keep you aware and therefore protected.

Ingredients

A pot of rose hip, hibiscus, and passion fruit tea
4 cups cranberry juice
3 blood oranges, sliced
Red rose petals

10 drops each of sweet orange and rose absolute essential oils
Obsidian, carnelian, and citrine crystals

Ritual

- Place all the ingredients in the bath at a temperature of your choosing.
- Light some candles.
- Create a smudge using cinnamon and palo santo by putting them in a nonflammable tray of some kind and igniting them. Waft the smoke around your body using a feather you have found.
- Step into the bath and dunk your head underwater.
- Place the carnelian and obsidian crystals by your feet.
- Place the citrine crystal on your forehead.
- In your mind's eye, focus on who or what you love most in this world. Try not to let your ego distract you from this powerful work for ten minutes.
- Open your eyes and focus on the reds of your bath. Imagine the water giving you a translucent shield of red light around your aura, sealing you in with the protection of awareness that comes from the power of love.
- Sit and soak in the powerful energy you've created.

Birth Bath

EAST, WIND, SPRING, GEMINI
TEA PAIRING: RED RASPBERRY AND NETTLE TEA

Red is the color of life. It is the color of family, our source of all life. Red is the color of birth. Giving birth is one of the most powerful ceremonies we can experience, and so it requires special preparation and care. This bath is perfect for this powerful rite of passage. Use it as a regular bath or a footbath. If you get the honor of being able to organize a blessingway (a celebration for a mother-to-be) for someone, prepare this as a footbath for them.

Ingredients

1 cup pink Himalayan sea salt

A pot of red raspberry tea

1 cup raspberry juice

1 cup red rose petals

1 cup pink rose petals

10 drops each of rose absolute and lavender
  essential oils

Rose quartz crystal

Ritual

- Place all the ingredients in the bath at a temperature of your choosing.
- Light some candles.
- Create a smudge using palo santo by putting it in a nonflammable tray of some kind and igniting it. Waft the smoke around your body using a feather you have found.
- Place your feet in the footbath or step into the bathtub.
- Sing a song that feels like trust for you, like power. Sing a song that feels like strength. If nothing comes to mind, simply open your mouth, relax your jaw, and release sounds from your belly up through your heart, through your throat, and out of your mouth.
- Soak in the medicine you've created.

Strength Bath

NORTH, EARTH, TAURUS, WINTER
TEA PAIRING: ROSE, CINNAMON, AND NETTLE TEA

All things red point back to strength: to release attachments, to give birth, to be aware, to get grounded, to find our home, and to learn the wisdom of our ancestors. All these endeavors take strength to initiate and give strength when completed. Sometimes we simply need the strength to surrender personal will (our ego) to the power of divine will (our love). This simple bath can help us find our strength and endurance.

Ingredients

3 cups Epsom salt

1 bunch of fresh rosemary sprigs

2 cups red rose petals

10 drops each of rose absolute and rosemary essential oils

Ruby crystal

Ritual

- Place all the ingredients in the bath at a temperature of your choosing.
- Light some candles.
- Create a smudge using white sage by putting it in a nonflammable tray of some kind and igniting it. Waft the smoke around your body using a feather you have found.
- Step into the bath and dunk your head underwater.
- Place the ruby crystal on your heart as a reminder of the power of your love.
- Ask the water to give you strength.
- Sit and soak in the medicine you've created.

2

Orange

Orange is the color of movement and momentum. The color of joy. When we call the color orange into our auras, we are seeking healthy relationships to money, food, partners, friends, and family. We want a fresh breath of air for our creative spirits.

THE LIGHT

Oranges are generally magnetic and fun-to-be-around people. They are attractive, even if they don't meet cultural beauty ideals. There is something sexy about them. They are effortlessly friendly and tend to have a lot of friends. Oranges have a lot of energy, especially for things they are interested in, and tend to be financially successful in creative careers. Highly fertile and highly creative, orange is the color of calling in our spirit babies. Orange people can attract just about anything to them and are meant to have an easy, graceful life.

THE SHADOW

The big word here is *control*. When Oranges are out of balance, they can be controlling about everything relationship based. At worst, this can lead to eating disorders and relationships where they are overly dominant toward their partner. Usually fine with change, Oranges in their shadow will try to change you to the vision they see fit for you, or for themselves. Oranges can be overly frugal, thinking that the money they now have is all the money they will ever have. They are the ones who show up at dinner with friends claiming to have forgotten their wallets. They can mask this control with a carefree manner, but underneath that go-with-the-flow attractive energy, they are gripping at every last penny, stressing about relationships, obsessing about their diets, and blocking themselves creatively.

ORANGE BATHS

CREATIVITY BATH

SEXUAL HEALING BATH

FOR ALL MY RELATIONSHIPS BATH

MONEY BATH

FORGIVENESS, CELEBRATION,
HAPPINESS BATH

FERTILITY BATH

Creativity Bath

WATER, EAST, CAPRICORN, GEMINI, CANCER, SUMMER
TEA PAIRING: CHAI TEA WITH BASIL

I believe that we are all born with creative spirits. It's the defining, conditioning, and categorizing that takes creativity and crushes it. So many children are amazing actors, artists, writers, or painters, and then they are told that they can't make a living doing what they love, so they go to school for something more "sensible." Later on in life, they find that their inner artists aren't satisfied with the stale bread and water they have been handed. If they are brave, they return to the truth of who they are. They start taking acting classes again or pick up watercolors. I often wonder how different things would be if young creative spirits were encouraged to express themselves in a world that supported them.

Orange is an amazing color to work with when you need to spark your creative fire. Sometimes we can feel a new idea coming, but for some reason we are blocked. Usually, it's our controlling ego that stops creative energy from coming in. Maybe we are too hung up on things needing to happen in a certain way. Maybe we can see the what, but we are being too specific about the how. Maybe we are parallel to our creative path, but not necessarily on it.

In the past two decades of offering Medicine Readings, I've noticed that blocked creative energy is the main source of depression. Your body, mind, and spirit want to express themselves a bit differently, but for some reason you are pressuring and trapping yourself. You speak about feeling stuck, which is exactly the feeling that blocked creative energy gives you. To heal this, you don't need to focus on the big masterpiece you are meant to create so much as the small creative changes in your life. Try making adjustments that break up the routine and the monotony. Even if it is something as small as taking a different route to work. Any little change you make will free up your creative energy and then inspire you to free up some more. This bath can help as well.

Ingredients

1 cup Epsom salt

3 oranges, sliced into rounds

Leaves from 1 bunch of fresh basil

3 cinnamon sticks

A pot of chai tea

One 8-ounce can coconut milk

10 drops each of vanilla and sweet orange essential oils

Citrine, moonstone, and carnelian crystals

The Dream: Vanilla bean orchids and a sapphire crystal

Ritual

- Place all the ingredients in the bath at a temperature of your choosing.
- Light a candle.
- Cleanse your aura with a selenite wand.
- Step into the bath and dunk your head underwater.
- Place a sapphire or moonstone crystal on your third eye.
- Place a citrine on your belly.
- Take ten deep powerful breaths, inhaling the scents of your bath.
- Release your jaw.
- Feel the energy, the pure energy, in your heart.
- Let that energy travel up your throat and out through your mouth, releasing the sound of your heart.
- Bathe in this sound. Bathe in the water.
- Ask all that you are soaking in and the light you carry within to send you creative inspiration.
- Soak in the medicine you've created.

Sexual Healing Bath

FIRE, EAST, SCORPIO, AUTUMN
TEA PAIRING: NETTLE, ROSE, AND PALO SANTO TEA

We can carry sexual wounding, shame, and trauma from our maternal and paternal lineages, past lives, and, of course, experiences and conditioning of this lifetime. In mainstream media, there is also a gross oversexualization of the female form, which leads to objectification. We need to understand how much harm objectification of any kind can cause. Women, in particular, have been treated as objects for far too long, and not just by men. Women objectify one another. As with so many issues that are being brought to light, the only way out of this is through it, and the way through is by sharing our stories and the wisdom we've gained. Your sexual history doesn't have to be a source of shame or pain. You can and will heal from anything. Even experiences like sexual trauma. I can give you strength and courage.

Objectification causes harm, and, in my experience, it leads to a strong fear of being seen, propelling a lot of us into feelings of isolation—or else we begin objectifying ourselves and using our sexuality to get what we want.

It is very difficult to have a balanced sexuality. Especially with what is being modeled for us in our society and the stories we carry with us from our ancestors. There are the dogmas of spirituality that teach abstinence is the way to enlightenment, but sexual repression can lead to a convoluted view on sexuality. And then there is the direct counter, the dogmas of spirituality, which teach polyamory and orgies are the way to enlightenment. These experiences usually leave people feeling energetically drained, heartbroken, and sick, because they've mistaken their sexuality for their power. Yes, your sexual energy is your creative energy. When you are exploiting yourself sexually, using sex as a weapon or as a tool for enlightenment, or sleeping with too many people, take notice of how you feel creatively. Notice how much work you are actually getting done, how much money you are actually making. Chances are that these energies are being drained along with the sexual energy that is being overused.

There is also the trap of staying in sexless and even loveless relationships because you have been conditioned to believe that this is what you are supposed to do. Sex is huge in relationships, and while I don't think you need to be having it all the time, I do think that connecting sexually with your partner in life is extremely important. If you are still physically healthy enough but are in a marriage that has given up on sex, ask yourself whether you are in the relationship for love or out of necessity.

I say choose the sexual journey that feels most like love to you. I can't tell you what that is for you; no one but you can. If you let self-love lead, chances are you will find balance and health in your mind, body, spirit, heart, and sex life.

Healthy sexual experiences can truly open you up, give you visions, and help you to know yourself better. I think it's important to know the extremes that are out there, and at the same time choose for yourself the sexual path that is best for you. Write a new sexual story for yourself, one that has not disregarded but integrated wisdom gained from the pain of the past, a new version of you that now has the strength and courage to truly be sexually happy. This bath is designed to help us arrive at our sexual truth.

Ingredients

1 cup Epsom salt

A pot of nettle tea

A handful of yellow rose petals

A pinch of mugwort leaves

10 drops of rosemary, 5 drops of vetiver, and 3 drops of patchouli essential oils

Labradorite crystal

Ritual

- Place all the ingredients in the bath at a temperature of your choosing.
- Light a candle and shut off all the lights in your bathroom.
- Create a smudge using palo santo by putting it in a nonflammable tray of some kind and igniting it. Waft the smoke around your body using a feather you have found.
- Step into the bath and dunk your head underwater.
- Take several deep, cleansing breaths. For ten minutes, stare into the flame of your candle and try not to blink, letting tears roll down your cheeks and merge with the water you're bathing in.

- Imagine yourself in the peak of sexuality. Who are you with? Where are you? What are you doing?
- Sit and soak in the cleansing energy you've created.

For All My Relationships Bath

EARTH, WEST, LEO, SCORPIO, TAURUS, SUMMER
TEA PAIRING: ROSE AND SAFFRON TEA

If you weren't blessed to have healthy relationships modeled for you when you were younger, creating healthy relationships in life can be very difficult. When people come in for a Medicine Reading, one of the things that gets discussed the most is relationships. I will start with the big one, which is our romantic relationships. We live in a culture that finds it impossible to be happy with what we have. For the most part, we are asking ourselves, "What's next?" rather than "What's now?" We can also treat our romantic relationships in this way. I think that if you are in a marriage and you are truly suffering, you must decide if it's best for you to continue this way or not. Most of the time I think it's really important to try to work it out.

Why?

Male or female, I think that we often are attracted to people who have a similar energy to our mothers. Our relationships with our mothers (if you were adopted this includes both birth mother and adoptive mother) are the most important we will ever have. Often we choose our mothers, and our spirits float around her waiting for the right time for us to come through. If we go through our whole childhood and teenage years not working through the shadow energy in the relationship with our mothers, we then choose partners who will give us another chance to learn and grow. This is why we are sometimes so deeply attracted to people whose words and actions cause us suffering. They are not making us suffer. We are choosing to suffer because that is what is needed in order for us to grow. You have to decide to be done with the suffering, decide that you are ready to grow, but that doesn't always mean be done with the relationship that you are in.

There are two practices I recommend for creating healthy relationships, whether romantic, familial, or platonic: confrontation and conscious connection. One of the things that can really hold us back from growing through our relating is when we are hurt or not speaking up for ourselves when something or someone is bringing us down. Most of us are afraid of confrontation, but I think that is a mistake. I think it is possible to

become spiritual and then think we've "let go," but in reality, that energy is getting stored up somewhere and will find its way out through our skin, our bellies, or an unnecessary outburst. Sometimes we wait years and years and have that confrontation from a place of calcified suffering.

I suggest when you are feeling hurt, rather than holding it in, let go of the fear of being uncomfortable and talk about it. Sometimes we need to consciously confront ourselves and really look at the choices we've been making that caused us harm. Sometimes we need to consciously confront a friend or family member, and sometimes we need to consciously confront our partners. We must tell them, in the moment or after taking a brief pause to put our anger and hurt in check, that something feels off. I don't believe we need to yell; I think it's important, no matter how hurt you are, to put yourself in the other's shoes and try to understand where they were coming from. I think that this is a place where you can really embrace being an empath, and your sensitivity is your strength. Take a deep breath, be brave, and confront.

Conscious connection can be just as difficult or scary as conscious confrontation. In our relationship with ourselves, homes, parents, children, friends, and romantic partners, it can be easy to just continue. It is easy to squeeze into the mold we've poured for ourselves and show up as the person others expect us to be rather than as our authentic selves. Connecting and reconnecting can give us the opportunity to have the courage to show up as ourselves and embrace the idea that we are constantly evolving human beings.

Ask your loved one to do something with you that feels like true connection, whether that's taking a walk, having a conversation, or engaging in more eye contact. You may find that when you are the first one who makes the move to consciously connect, your partner has really been craving it too.

There's a reason we humans need to have relationships in order to continue life. Relationships are hard work, yes, but they also help us to grow. And really, the only thing we are here to do is grow. We're here to make things better for future generations. This bath may not heal all of your relationships in twenty minutes, but it might give you a moment to connect to the creative inspiration you have within you and help you grow alongside the people you love, through conscious confrontation and conscious connection.

Ingredients

1 cup Epsom salt

1 cup ocean water

1 cup water that has caught the full moon light

1 tablespoon apple cider vinegar

A pot of saffron tea

Fresh white pine needles

A handful of pink rose petals

10 drops of rose absolute and 5 drops of patchouli essential oils

Rose quartz crystal

Ritual

- Place all the ingredients in the bath at a temperature of your choosing.
- Light a candle.
- Create a smudge using palo santo by putting it in a nonflammable tray of some kind and igniting it. Waft the smoke around your body using a feather you have found.
- Step into your bath and dunk your head underwater.
- Place the rose quartz crystal on your belly.
- Scan your body for any place where you are holding relationship tension. Pay extra attention to your joints.
- If you find any relationship tension in your body, where is it coming from? What can you do to heal that relationship?
- Take a long time with this bath.
- Sit and soak in the magic of the medicine you've created.

Money Bath

EARTH, NORTH, AQUARIUS, SUMMER
TEA PAIRING: TULSI TEA

One of my and my husband's new year intentions was to take a year to focus on being happy with what we have.

We decided that if we really want to do things like move apartments and one day buy a house, we first needed to get out of debt, start a savings account, and build great credit. And above all of these things, we most importantly needed to be able to appreciate and take care of what we already have.

The truth is, I didn't really know how to "make friends with money." I had not been willing to sit with my discomfort around money, which I picked up from historically not having any, to start paying closer attention to my finances. I've always worked very hard (for example, this whole book is mostly being written at around four o'clock in the morning before I begin a full day of mom-ing and Medicine Readings). I've had what most would call an incredible amount of success in my business, yet I had never taken time to celebrate that success. I felt that if I did, the success would become real, and then the other shoe might drop. So I just kept focusing on working harder and "What's next?" I knew I would have to do a lot of self-reflection if I was truly going to be my own financial healer.

After setting this new year intention of being happy with what we have, I began reading all of the financial books I could get my hands on. I learned so much. I also recognized that because I had spent almost no time in my life focusing on financial well-being, I could probably use some help. So I hired a financial organizer. From there, I started understanding when it was a safe time to invest more into growing my business, and when it made more sense to sit tight and be patient. Money is just an energy, after all. I can understand energy, so I can understand money too. By taking the pressure off looking at money as all powerful, I was able to start becoming friends with it and treating it as just another energy in this infinite universe.

Something interesting starting happening as well. The things I wanted but wasn't buying for myself just started being sent to me—like new clothes, jewelry, shoes, beauty products, even a holiday in Mexico for the family—through the success of my business. It was as though through being happy with what I have, I attracted more abundance, and specifically more money, into my life. I started having financial confidence or maybe just more confidence in general. Yes, I can see I am human with a lot to learn, and I'm going to choose to love myself through it.

Honestly, we didn't totally stick to the being happy with what we have yearlong challenge. When I paid off all our debt, we celebrated by leasing a car (I learned through the financial books I was reading that this was a write-off because I own my own business). I got the boots that I'd been eyeing for a long time. But for the most part we stuck to groceries, our daughter's needs, and gifts for each other's birthdays or our anniversary.

Throughout the year I was creating and investing in my Ritual Bath Kit, a necessary but costly growth in my business, and because of my newfound friendship with money I was able to use the medicine of being happy with what I have. I took time to pause, look around me, and celebrate the success that had already come. From this place of positivity, I felt confident, mo-

tivated, and capable. That energy spread throughout my company to successfully launch the Ritual Bath Kit. The launch did so well that I made back the money I had invested within the first week.

The medicine of being happy with what I have, the medicine of gratitude, has given me so much. Instead of looking at my personal life, my business, even my spiritual life, with scarcity and saying, "What's next?" I now look at it more like "How can we benefit the most from the gifts I've already been given?"

The medicine of being happy with what I have helped me to answer questions such as "What do I really want?" Yes, I want to move into a different home, but it doesn't have to be today or even this year. It also answered a big question for us: Should we have another child? We looked at our family, how happy we all are, and said this is enough.

The sweetest part of taking the year to be happy with what we have was that my husband and I are having the most successful year in our relationship to date. We realized that if we have enough, and if I am enough, and you are enough, then we are enough for each other.

I think we will keep the intention of working on being happy with what we have mov-

ing forward. I know that I still have so much to learn from it, and I'm excited to see what comes from more of this sweet medicine. This bath is designed to give you a moment to celebrate exactly where you are and reap the fruits of what you have sown. Go ahead and celebrate. You are worth it.

Ingredients

1 cup Epsom salt

1 cup orange juice

1 cup peach juice

1 cup coconut milk

Fresh basil leaves

3 fresh peaches, sliced

Pink rose petals

Moss agate, malachite, emerald, and
    citrine crystals

Ritual

- Place all the ingredients in the bath at a temperature of your choosing.
- Light a candle.
- Create a smudge using a cinnamon stick by putting it in a nonflammable tray of some kind and igniting it. Waft the smoke around your body using a feather you have found.
- Step into the bath and dunk your head underwater.
- Close your eyes and place both hands on your belly.
- Take a deep breath and, in your mind's eye, see yourself exactly as you are sitting here in this bath, soaking in the water, with all these beautiful plants and stones around you.
- From that big beautiful heart of yours, send a wave of gratitude out for this moment. Breathe into that feeling.
- Then travel to the unseen aspects of this moment for you. Your home, the money that you do have, your belongings, your work, your family, your plants, and your precious animals. From that big beautiful heart of yours, send a wave of gratitude out for this moment. And breathe into that space.
- And again.
- And again.
- Sit and soak in the medicine you've created.

Forgiveness, Celebration, Happiness Bath

SOUTH, EARTH, SUMMER, GEMINI, LIBRA
TEA PAIRING: LEMON BALM TEA

What does it truly mean to be happy? Why is happiness one of the most fabricated, faked, and marketed emotions? Do we all truly want to be happy?

The four deadly poisons that wipe out happiness are comparison, attachment, expectation, and shame. I think true happiness is a life of balance, a life of fulfillment, a life of realizing how very little we need but having those needs met, a life of healthy relationships.

It is not realistic for people to expect themselves to be happy all the time. We all have ups and downs, highs and lows. People who can live happily will experience the full spectrum of feelings, but they will not attach or necessarily identify themselves with any of these feelings. They won't even necessarily identify themselves as happy. They go through hard times, they feel sadness and anger, but they integrate these experiences as lessons learned and move on. Repression = depression. Happiness comes when we truly feel we are free to be and express ourselves.

I highly suggest not expecting anyone or anything outside of yourself to bring you happiness. That will almost always go wrong and will almost always be a fork in the rib of your relationships. No one is responsible for your happiness except you. Your parents, your partner, and your friends are all just other beings trying to find happiness themselves. Look at the ways in which you are holding yourself back from finding happiness and work your way out from there.

One of the biggest ways we prevent happiness from thriving in our lives is comparison. The moment you begin to compare yourself to others you will find that whatever happiness you felt before has evaporated. Check yourself: When are you doing the most comparing? If you find when you go on social media you start comparing yourself to others, follow only accounts that truly inspire you or that you think are purposeful for you. Letting go of social media completely or from time to time can be powerful. Check

whether you compare yourself with the people in your life. Try to appreciate them for who they are, and remember we are all on our own paths.

You need not have shame for who you are, what you've done in your past, or what you've been through. All of these experiences bring you to where you are today. You have great purpose here. Your unique spirit and its history have medicine to bring to this planet. Guilt, regret, and shame will only hold you back and weigh you down.

Don't drink the deadly poisons of comparison, attachment, expectation, and shame; instead, be brave and really listen to your needs. Make sure that they are met, and then let yourself feel fulfilled and content with who you are. You may not be able to change where you've been, but it's up to you to decide where you will go.

Follow the wise voice of your inner child. If you feel depressed, be honest with yourself and ask the questions: Have I truly been outside enough? Into nature enough? Go swing

on a swing, jump rope, ride a bike, tell someone how much you love them, pick some flowers for a friend, or paint with watercolors—not because you want to make a masterpiece but because it's fun to paint. Instead of buying stuff, fix and repurpose what you already have. Try these things and see how you feel. This bath is designed to help you to feel so happy that you sparkle.

Ingredients

1 cup red alaea sea salt

1 cup oat milk

1 tablespoon copper powder

A pot of saffron tea

A tub tea of lemon balm, linden, violet, rose hip, and St. John's wort

White rose petals

Clear quartz crystal

3 drops each of jasmine, linden blossom, and sweet orange essential oils

The Dream: Jasmine and linden flowers

Ritual

- Place all the ingredients in the bath at a temperature of your choosing.
- Light a candle.
- Put on some peaceful but happy music.
- Create a smudge using sweetgrass by putting it in a nonflammable tray of some kind and igniting it. Waft the smoke around your body using a feather you have found.
- Step into the bath and dunk your head underwater.
- Place the clear quartz crystal on your heart.
- Ask the water to remind you of your joy.
- Ask the water to teach you how to be receptive to joy.
- Ask the water to guide your visions toward one thing you can do to evoke happiness.
- Sit and soak in the medicine you've created.

Fertility Bath

EAST, SPRING, EARTH, CANCER, SCORPIO, VIRGO
TEA PAIRING: RED CLOVER AND WAYUSA TEA

Fertility is such a personal journey for everyone. "Shoulds" do not apply here. As you clear away the ovary-blocking poisons of judgment and comparison, you can come into a place of patience and understand that you are on a profound journey to one of the most powerful rites of passage possible.

In my practice, I would say about 40 percent of the people who come in are women who are trying to conceive. When they come, I look to see if they have a spirit baby in their auras, and if so, if there are any signs the spirit baby wants to communicate in order for him or her to come through. Sometimes it is emotional work, like the mother-to-be needing to forgive her own mother, and sometimes the mother-to-be needs to simply make space in her home, life, and schedule so the baby can see that the mom has time for them. Most of the time, babies don't come exactly when we want them to.

I had one client who came in at the age of forty and it took her another five years to get pregnant. When clients who want to have a child come to me, they do not all have spirit babies around them, but that doesn't mean that they will not get pregnant. It just means that the baby isn't showing up for them in that Medicine Reading because there are other aspects of the spirit, of the aura, that need to be unpacked before we can really get into the energy of the baby. Some people come in with ten or fifteen spirit babies around them; some will land Earth side and some will be working with them on the spiritual plane.

It's a little different for all of us, but if we are brave enough to face what could be blocking our babies from coming through, then chances are we are in the right moment to conceive. The key ingredient for fertility is receptivity. If our doors are closed and our minds are fixed, how can anyone get in? What if a baby wants to come, but not how or when you want them to? Can you be okay with that? Will you have the courage to stay open and receptive even if you are disappointed?

I look back at the time when I thought I was physically blocked from getting pregnant and realize it was just that so many things had to come into alignment before giving birth. I had to come into alignment in order to call in the spirit of this beautiful baby girl. I think our spirit babies find us and they wait for the right time to come through. She didn't want my ex to be her father. She knew her dad and waited for us to find each other. I almost wonder if it was her energy that made everything feel so magical when her father and I first met. I give thanks to the plants in the brew that melted my fibroids and increased my fertility. I give thanks to my teacher who felt called to ask me if I ever wanted to have kids. I give thanks to the universe and the divine timing of all in this life.

This bath includes some of the plants I was bathing in on my *dieta* (or their North American equivalents) before I became pregnant. This ritual emulates the work I was doing myself in order to tell the spirit of my beautiful daughter that it was time for her to come through.

Ingredients

1 cup salt

A pot of wayusa tea

A pot of red clover tea

3 peaches, sliced

Epsom salt

Pink rose petals

Fresh rosemary

Rose quartz and citrine crystal

3 drops each of rose and rosemary
   essential oils

1 cup small-batch, special, local raw honey

The Dream: Fresh wayusa leaves, grape leaves,
   and red clover flowers

Ritual

- Place all the ingredients in the bath at a temperature of your choosing.
- Light a candle.
- Create a smudge using mugwort by putting it in a nonflammable tray of some kind and igniting it. Waft the smoke around your body using a feather you have found.
- Step into the bath and dunk your head underwater.
- Place the rose quartz on your heart with an intention of receptivity.
- Place the citrine on your womb with the intention of nourishment.
- Connect to the spirit of your unborn ones. Ask them to give you guidance about anything you may need to do in preparation for their arrival. The answer may not come right away; it may come in the next few days in signs, the way our spirit speaks to us.
- Offer patience to yourself and your future baby
- Sit and soak in the medicine you've created.

3

Yellow

There can be so many shades of yellow in the aura. A bright lemon yellow usually means joy and an ability to healthily digest experiences, food, and whatever one may need to take in. A strong cadmium yellow means a strong sense of self and trust in one's own instincts. I get worried about people when I see yellow ocher around them, because to me it signifies addiction.

THE LIGHT

Yellows are bright! Yellows are fast learners, advancing in academia with ease. They also love to read and tend to be quite curious. They are not afraid to ask hard questions for the sake of research. Yellows make excellent reporters, journalists, and engineers. If ever I needed brain surgery, I would want a Yellow to be my surgeon. When they are learning, they are happy. This is true for a five-year-old Yellow as much as it is for one who is eighty-five. Yellows crave joy, they seek it out in everything they do. Confident in who they are and with a strong sense of self, Yellows will be the first to raise their hands when offered an opportunity and have no shame about getting called to the front of the line. As natural competitors, we can also see Yellows in their element when they are engaged in sports, board games, or anything that could in any way offer them a chance to show their bravado and skill. Still, Yellows value friendship above all and usually keep friends for a lifetime. They are active in their communities and make strangers feel welcome.

THE SHADOW

Yellow can change shades when it gets into its shadow and here is unfortunately where we face addiction. Drugs can steal our spirits and our sense of self. When we lose ourselves in addiction, we become whatever we are addicted to. When I see people addicted to gossip, drugs, or shopping, I see a yellow ocher around them. Yellows in their shadow use their intelligence to get what they want and can turn very manipulative. They will have no problem lying about who they are or using others for their own gain. Sense of self can get caught up in image and they can appear as egotistical know-it-alls.

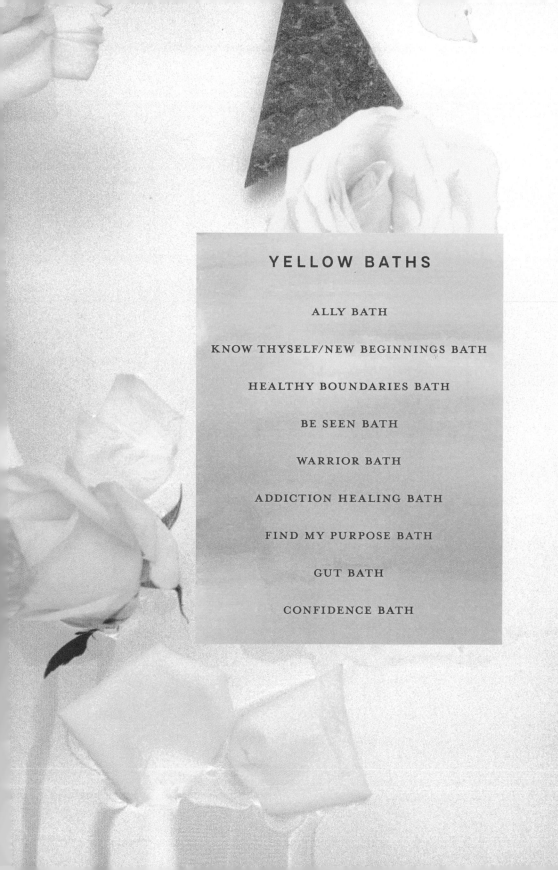

YELLOW BATHS

ALLY BATH

KNOW THYSELF/NEW BEGINNINGS BATH

HEALTHY BOUNDARIES BATH

BE SEEN BATH

WARRIOR BATH

ADDICTION HEALING BATH

FIND MY PURPOSE BATH

GUT BATH

CONFIDENCE BATH

Ally Bath

EAST, SPRING, EARTH, GEMINI, ARIES
TEA PAIRING: NETTLE, LEMON BALM, AND ROSE TEA

We have allies everywhere: in a dear sweet and supportive friend, in the family we are born into or create, in the pets we love, in artists who inspire us, in the clairsentient writers of songs and poems who are communicating exactly what is in our hearts, in Great Spirit, and in Mother Nature and all of her magnificent creations.

Spending time embraced by these allies is such restorative medicine. It becomes harder and harder to make friends as we grow older and go through major rites of passage in life like marriage, childbirth, losing a loved one, moving cities, or changing jobs. We tend to lose touch with some friends. This isn't because they no longer love us, but because as our experiences diverge, we may not be able to understand what the other has been through as we once did. To add to that, our smartphone culture has us feeling more and more isolated and lonely. We can see what the people we know are up to without ever actually reaching out to them, and because people mostly post only the good stuff, it's easy to feel as if everyone else has a happier, better life than you do.

If you've lost touch with a friend, be the brave one who reaches out and reconnects. Let go of any perceived judgment they may have about you. Better yet, create experiences that gather friends together. Start doing your own moon ceremonies and sharing circles. Write down the dreams that you have each night, and then gather together in community to share them.

Instead of feeling wounded by old friendships, heal them. As we become more sensitive, we have to be careful we don't become the sacred asshole. Just because your old family and friends can't connect with your spiritual interests doesn't mean you can't spend time with them. You may not want to go to happy hour anymore, but it's important to find new ways——be it a movie or a walk——to consciously connect. This doesn't mean hiding or lowering your own frequency. Instead, show up lovingly for yourself and your companion, setting an example through the consciousness you cultivate in your life.

This bath contains some of my most beloved allies—my plant and stone friends. I want to share them with you because I think you will find they are sweet friends to us all.

Ingredients

1 cup Epsom salt
A pinch of evening primrose
A pinch of echinacea
2 pinches of nettles
2 pinches of lemon balm
1 pinch of black-eyed Susan

Yellow rose petals
10 drops of patchouli essential oil
Clear quartz crystal
Jade crystals
The Dream: Fresh evening primrose flowers

Ritual

- Place all the ingredients in the bath at a temperature of your choosing.
- Light a candle.
- Create a smudge using sweetgrass by putting it in a nonflammable tray of some kind and igniting it. Waft the smoke around your body using a feather you have found.
- Step into the bath and dunk your head underwater.
- Close your eyes and imagine the friendliest examples nature gives us (for me it's puppies).
- Invite all your spirit allies to surround you.
- Invite receptivity to meeting more allies.
- Sit and soak in the sweet medicine you've created.

Know Thyself/New Beginnings Bath

FIRE, EAST, SPRING, CAPRICORN
TEA PAIRING: NETTLE, VIOLET LEAF AND FLOWER,
AND LINDEN BLOSSOM TEA

You can mourn what is behind you, but remember you must let it go to make room for the many blessings that want to come your way. In creating my business each step of the way I was asked to let go of my scarcity consciousness, to let go of my lack of self-worth, and simply own that I have a lot of work to do here in my time on this planet. Why not get started right away?

In terms of self-worth, my biggest challenge was having to let go of the way I did business before. In the past, I had focused on building others up rather than myself. I knew that in order to do the work that I was meant for, I was going to have to be okay with allowing myself to grow as large as possible, and be heard as loudly as possible; only through allowing myself to be seen would I be able to help others feel a little less alone, a little more supported, and able to understand that they are their own healers. That is why Space had to be birthed in New York City, a city where dreams are birthed and rebirthed four million times over on a daily basis.

And have you ever been to NYC in the spring? The beauty of the city is amplified. Light pink redbuds, apple and cherry blossoms, and yellow forsythia complement the unending scales of gray and the diffused lighting of the city, promising us rebirth and the end of the winter-long rest.

In certain schools of spiritual thought, spring is believed to be the hardest time of year because of the equal balance of light and shadow. But it doesn't have to be. It just depends on your ability to own your shadow while choosing your light. Let the full moons and rising sun amplify your ability to regenerate yourself. Begin again.

Full moons are a revelatory energy. When these revelations come it can be very powerful and profound to write them down. Very often when we revisit these entries later, we connect surprising dots, joining pieces that lead to profound insights and exciting rebirth. This bath is designed to help you bask in the full moon revelations of rebirth.

Ingredients

1 cup Epsom salt

A pot or tub tea of violet leaf and flower, cherry blossoms, and forsythia flower

One 8-ounce can coconut milk

A few drops of frangipani essential oil

Amethyst crystal

Citrine crystal

Rose quartz crystal

Ritual

- Place all the ingredients in the bath at a temperature of your choosing.
- Cleanse your aura with a selenite wand.
- Step into the bath and dunk your head underwater.
- Say or sing "Renew, regenerate, rebirth" into the water three times.
- Sit and soak in the powerful energy you've created.

Healthy Boundaries Bath

FIRE, WEST, SPRING, LEO

TEA PAIRING: ORANGE PEEL AND ROSE TEA OR A GLASS OF RED WINE

The power of this bath pulls the energy of your wild, passionate, and loving soul essence, your inner child, to the surface. Gift this bath to yourself when you need to release unwanted or unnecessary boundaries. Call in the new boundaries you wish to create that will allow you to do exactly what is best for you. Eliminate that which no longer serves you. Eliminate the presence of fear and stagnation and invite in clarity and purity. When you know who you are, you know who you are not. We are unity consciousness, we are everything and everyone. But that doesn't mean we need to process emotions for others or take responsibility for others' actions; that is disempowering, not just for you, but for those you're "helping" as well. Instead, take responsibility for yourself and your own actions. Know that by doing so, the tiny drop in the ocean of this family of sentient beings is feeling the ripples of the high vibrations you are creating. Lead by example. This bath is designed to help you decipher what is and is not your responsibility.

Ingredients

1 cup Epsom salt

A handful of pink rose petals

1 bottle of red wine

20 drops of sweet orange and 5 drops of jasmine essential oils

Carnelian crystal

Ritual

- Place all the ingredients in the bath at a temperature of your choosing.
- Light a candle.
- Create a smudge using a cinnamon stick by putting it in a nonflammable tray of some kind and igniting it. Waft the smoke around your body using a feather you have found.
- Step into the bath and dunk your head underwater.
- Place your crystal on your belly button.
- Talk to your inner child, saying "You are enough" three times.
- Soak in all the energy you have created.

Be Seen Bath

FIRE, SOUTH, SUMMER, LEO
TEA PAIRING: JASMINE GREEN TEA

Ingredients

1 cup sea salt

1 cup Epsom salt

1 cup blue green protein

A pot of green tea

A pot of tea made with fresh or dried rosemary

A handful of red rose petals

1 cucumber, sliced

2 or 3 cinnamon sticks

A handful of farmers' market flowers

5 drops each of rosemary and rose
    essential oils

Turquoise crystal

Jade crystal

Citrine or topaz crystal

Ritual

- Place all the ingredients in the bath at a temperature of your choosing.
- Cleanse your aura with a selenite wand.
- Step into the bath and dunk your head underwater.
- Place the turquoise crystal on your chest over your lungs.
- Breathe deeply into your heart center.
- Sing. Opening up your throat and singing is a powerful way to set the love that wants to work through you free. The song on page 104 is a medicine song that was first found by John Lomax in 1939 and it is so woven into the collective consciousness that we all know it well. Sing it to your inner child and the desire for the love within us to be seen that we all share in the collective consciousness.

This little light of mine, I'm gonna let it shine
This little light of mine, I'm gonna let it shine
This little light of mine, I'm gonna let it shine
Let it shine, shine, shine
Let it shine!

Everywhere I go, I'm gonna let it shine
Everywhere I go, I'm gonna let it shine
Everywhere I go, I'm gonna let it shine
Let it shine, shine, shine
Let it shine!

This little light of mine, I'm gonna let it shine
This little light of mine, I'm gonna let it shine
This little light of mine, I'm gonna let it shine
Let it shine, shine, shine
Let it shine!

All up in my house, I'm gonna let it shine
All up in my house, I'm gonna let it shine
All up in my house, I'm gonna let it shine
Let it shine, shine, shine
Let it shine!

This little light of mine, I'm gonna let it shine
This little light of mine, I'm gonna let it shine
This little light of mine, I'm gonna let it shine
Let it shine, shine, shine
Let it shine!

Out there in the dark
I'm gonna let it shine

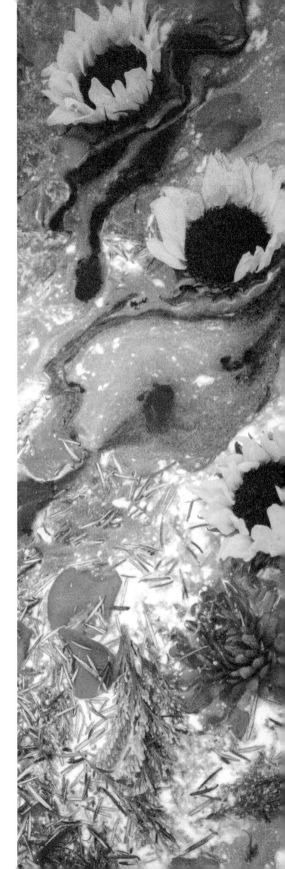

Out there in the dark
I'm gonna let it shine
Out there in the dark
I'm gonna let it shine
Let it shine, shine, shine
Let it shine!

This little light of mine, I'm gonna let it shine
This little light of mine, I'm gonna let it shine
This little light of mine
I'm gonna let it shine
Let it shine, shine, shine
Let it shine!

[OUTRO]

Let it shine, shine, shine
Let it shine!
Let it shine, shine, shine
Let it shine!

- Imagine yourself surrounded by a brilliant golden green light that supports you with all the protection and love Mother Nature has to offer. From this supported place she asks you what it is within you that you've always had. Write how this light of yours that has always been can work to help the healing of our human family, the light you have that can help you to heal yourself.
- Sit and soak in the medicine you've created.

Warrior Bath

FIRE, SOUTH, SUMMER, CAPRICORN
TEA PAIRING: OOLONG TEA

Warriors become warriors not from reacting to past trauma, but through integrating past experiences into their understanding of who they are today. They know and trust themselves. They aren't afraid to stand up for what they feel is right.

Be a warrior of love and truth. Don't let any mold that has been made for you make you forget the truth of who you are. You are love embodied. The full moon is a great opportunity to allow your true warrior's purpose to be revealed to you. Find the symbols in nature of those who are so profoundly comfortable being who they are—like our sister the moon, up there in her power, shining bright and guiding us with her light—and learn from them. Weave her story into the essence of your being. This bath is the perfect tool for this practice.

Ingredients

1 cup Epsom salt

3 oranges, sliced

5 sunflowers

Collected wildflowers (optional)

10 drops of sweet orange and 5 drops of patchouli essential oils

Tangerine quartz crystal

Labradorite crystal

Citrine crystals

Ritual

- Place all the ingredients in the bath at a temperature of your choosing.
- Create a smudge using cinnamon sticks and palo santo by putting them in a nonflammable tray of some kind and igniting them. Waft the smoke around your body using a feather you have found.
- Step into the bath and dunk your head underwater.
- Focus and reflect on the times in your life when you've been a warrior. This can be as simple as the fact that you cleared time for yourself to take this bath.
- Close your eyes, soak, enjoy, sing to the water, and bless yourself, so you can set an example of light to all.

Addiction Healing Bath

WIND, WEST, AUTUMN, CANCER
TEA PAIRING: KAVA, OSHA ROOT, GOLDENROD, DANDELION, LEMON BALM,
CHRYSANTHEMUM, VALERIAN, YARROW, AND ST. JOHN'S WORT TEA

Addiction is a very serious and often misunderstood issue. I am one of many who have lost someone close to them because of it. No matter what the substance or habit of choice, the color all addicts have in common is yellow ocher. This is the color of inverted will. The color that appears when your ego is working against you. I personally have tried speaking up about it many times, but in the end an addict will really stop using only if they want to. The truth is that some people don't want to heal. They are too attached to their pain. Sometimes because of their upbringing and the history of their spirit, they confuse suffering for love.

If you are suffering from addiction of any kind, know that you are not empty, there is not a void within you that needs to be filled with some substance, person, habit, or pattern. I know it is hard, but only you can choose to break the cycle.

I can recommend a bath for you, but the bath won't work, nothing will work, if you don't have the willpower. *You* have to choose to stand up for yourself. *You* have to find yourself again and move past letting the addiction define you. Get the help you need, maybe seeking professional help and reaching out to people who love you to let them know how much you're struggling.

Take responsibility and hold yourself accountable. It is so very disempowering to blame your addiction on someone else or on something that has happened to you. By realizing you are an active participant in wounding yourself, you can also choose to no longer participate in that which hurts you. If you are ready to let it, love will heal you. It will fill you up with something more powerful than any drug or habit.

This bath is designed to help you come home to yourself and release addiction.

Ingredients

5 cups Epsom salt

A tub tea of kava, osha root, goldenrod, dandelion, lemon balm, chrysanthemum, valerian, yarrow, and St. John's wort

Fresh dandelion flowers, daffodils, yellow rose petals, chrysanthemum flowers, yarrow flowers, and St. John's wort flowers

1 lemon, sliced

1 tablespoon apple cider vinegar

1 tablespoon baking soda

10 drops of frangipani and 5 drops of lemon balm essential oils

Smoky quartz, citrine, carnelian, rose quartz, obsidian, and clear quartz crystals

The Dream: Frangipani flowers

Ritual

- Place all the ingredients in the bath at a temperature of your choosing.
- Light a candle.
- Put on some very soothing music.
- Create a smudge using white cedar by putting it in a nonflammable tray of some kind and igniting it. Waft the smoke around your body using a feather you have found.
- Step into the bath and dunk your head underwater.
- Place the smoky quartz crystal on your belly.
- Place the citrine crystal on your left hip.
- Place the carnelian crystal on your right hip.
- Place the rose quartz on your heart.
- Hold the obsidian crystal in your left hand.
- Hold the clear quartz in your right hand.
- Take three deep breaths.
- Then find a rhythmic breathing of two inhales through the nose and one exhale out of the mouth.
- Keep breathing like this for the extent of two songs, or about ten minutes, taking breaks whenever you need to. After this, let go of all control on your breathing. Allow deep sighs to release from your open mouth, as if your belly and your heart are sighing.

- Ask the water to heal you. Ask the water to help you cleanse the grip of the substance you are abusing.
- Trust that you will heal.
- Set a vow of accountability and responsibility for yourself. Hold up the clear quartz crystal and say this vow into the crystal, infusing it with this intention. Later, sleep with and carry the crystal around with you wherever you go.
- Sit and soak in the magic and medicine you've created.

Find My Purpose Bath

EARTH, NORTH, SPRING, VIRGO, TAURUS
TEA PAIRING: ROSE AND BASIL TEA

In Medicine Readings, people often tell me they want to find their purpose. Maybe our purpose, the reason we all come into human form, is to grow. We grow toward becoming more and more loving. So, no matter what your occupation may be today, your ultimate purpose is to grow. There is a major difference between purpose and occupation. To be in alignment with our purpose, we simply need to allow the divine to work through us. We need to listen to divine will versus personal will. When personal will is working, there are a lot of *I have to*s and *I should*s. We can feel angst, and be stressed and uncertain. When it is divine will working through us, things may move a little more slowly, but rather than feeling overly nervous or excited, you will have a strong sense of peace. Things will flow and click together. You will feel you have angels looking out for you and helping you along the way.

If you feel overly nervous about something you are about to launch or a job you are about to take and things keep on somehow getting blocked, you are also being assisted by your angels. It's just that your personal will doesn't see it that way. You start to get frustrated and defeated and wonder why things never quite work out for you.

This is often when people turn to manifestation techniques like writing down every-thing they want specifically. This is where Yellows' bright intellect can think they know better than the divine. Is what we want what we need? If you are telling the universe that you want something specifically, are you also telling the universe I know better than you? Are you really being trusting and patient in that moment, or are you being demanding and rushing?

When we are in alignment with our purpose, which plain and simply means that we are growing toward being more and more loving and kind, we can manifest just about anything. You will think of something you need and—poof—it will appear. A small ex-ample of this is one day, I was telling my husband how much I felt called to go to Morocco. The very next day someone who organizes retreats in Morocco reached out to see if I would lead a retreat there.

When we mistake our purpose for our career, we will often change jobs, start businesses and not really pursue them, or begin an education in a certain field and not finish it. But when we realize that our purpose is to grow, and specifically to grow more loving, we tap into an abundance of energy, which will bring clarity to the job that will help us fulfill our work in this world. That is our purpose.

We all have different rivers of purpose that flow into the large and vast ocean of love. If you are having a hard time getting clear on how you are meant to grow and flow, try creating a practice of kindness. Start opening doors for others and saying please and thank you. Begin by helping others and doing your part. This will activate the energy of love and soon you will find your way. Just don't ever give up. It gets hard sometimes when we don't know exactly where we are going, but think of the river; she has no idea that she will become the ocean, yet she still can find her way around or through just about anything. The only thing that feels true for her is to flow. This bath is designed for you to soak in the power of your purpose.

Ingredients

1 cup Epsom salt

1 cup oat milk

1 lemon, sliced

Fresh basil leaves

Yellow rose petals

10 drops of sweet orange essential oil

Citrine crystal

Ritual

- Place all the ingredients in the bath at a temperature of your choosing.
- Light a candle.
- Create a smudge using copal by putting it in a nonflammable tray of some kind and igniting it. Waft the smoke around your body using a feather you have found.
- Cleanse your aura again with a selenite wand.
- Step into the bath and dunk your head underwater.
- Place the citrine crystal on your belly.
- Take a moment to surrender personal to divine will in your own way.
- Understand that personal will is there only to work for what divine will wants to do through you.
- Vow to let your instincts guide your intellect.
- Soak for a while in this intention and medicine you've created.

Gut Bath

EAST, WIND, AUTUMN, VIRGO
TEA PAIRING: SLIPPERY ELM AND CHAMOMILE TEA

Around 2014, I started noticing more and more people coming in with severe gut issues. Across the board, I noticed that they almost always had a base color of yellow gathered, mostly around their heads. They were bright, intelligent, caring, and overwhelmed. They were feeling very frustrated and disappointed in themselves for not feeling well because they felt they took such good care of themselves. They couldn't figure out what was wrong with them.

But with all of that energy in their heads and having so much they were figuring out all the time, how could energy go to the rest of their bodies?

When people go through intense experiences such as breakups, trauma, plant medicine ceremonies, taking antibiotics or other pharmaceutical drugs, losing a loved one, changing location, or other major life event, there is a lot of energy to process. This also happens when we are learning something new, going to school, or apprenticing. When we are taking in a lot of information in terms of energy mixing—for example, one day an acupuncture session, the next a Reiki session—there are a lot of mixed messages to process.

Whenever we have a lot of energy to digest, we need time to integrate and rest in order to properly assimilate. If we continue to stack experience on top of experience, we aren't taking the time to assimilate. That wreaks havoc on the physical body's processing system, the gut.

Sometimes our guts don't feel well so we get a bunch of tests, try different supplements, and learn as much as we can about how to heal. We go into be-your-own-healer over-drive. But learning and processing are two different things, and when we spend all our energy learning how to process, we are not actually giving ourselves a moment to process all the information that is coming in, and may even be making ourselves feel worse. My advice is to get out of your head into nature and your surroundings. Simplify your life. Take a break from electronics. Get enough rest. Then see how you feel. This very simple bath is designed to help you process.

Ingredients

1 cup Epsom salt

A pot of chamomile tea

Daisies

Clear quartz crystal

10 drops of lavender essential oil

Unscented candle

Ritual

- Place all the ingredients in the bath at a temperature of your choosing.
- Light the unscented candle.
- Cleanse your aura with a selenite wand.
- Step into the bath and dunk your head underwater.
- Place healing hands on your belly.
- Focus on the color yellow and send it through your hands into your belly for twenty minutes.
- Sit and soak in the magic you've created.

Confidence Bath

FIRE, SOUTH, SUMMER, LEO, SCORPIO, CAPRICORN
TEA PAIRING: SAFFRON AND ROSE TEA

If I could teach my daughter only one thing in this lifetime, it would be confidence. Let her discover that by believing in and knowing herself, by trusting how love wants to work through her, that she can do anything. I can only guide her to this through the example I set. Taking deep breaths and reminding myself that I was made for all the gifts that come into my life to support me as I let love flow through me; trying to remember that I worked hard for this, that I am worthy of all this and all the medicine it brings into my life.

What will it take for us to stop hiding? How can we give up our fear of being seen? How can we confidently say I am proud of who I have become?

Yes, we carry collective shame. Maybe because of past lives, we are afraid of persecution; but staying hidden doesn't help us grow. If we truly want to have confidence, we must know and embrace who we are. We must embrace our light and shadow. We must honor the growing we have done and that we are still doing. Confidence comes from knowing ourselves.

You do not have the same path as those around you. Even when it comes to those who are in the same field as you, you have your unique gifts and talents. Don't ingest the deadly poison of comparison; get out there, know who you are, embrace who you are, and shine, baby!

This bath is designed to help us know ourselves, embrace ourselves, and have confidence in who we are. Maybe that won't all come through in one day, but this bath is a way of showing yourself that you are committed to the process of self-discovery.

Ingredients

1 cup red alaea sea salt

A pot of saffron tea

1 cup coconut milk

Yellow rose petals

5 drops each of vetiver and patchouli essential oils

10 drops each of rose absolute and lavender essential oils

Your favorite non-water-soluble stones

Ritual

- Place all the ingredients in the bath at a temperature of your choosing.
- Light a candle.
- Create a smudge using palo santo by putting it in a nonflammable tray of some kind and igniting it. Waft the smoke around your body using a feather you have found.
- Step into the bath and dunk your head underwater.
- One at a time, hold your crystals in your hand. Ask them to help you self-reflect. Feel your unity with these stones, and the way we are all connected through the power of love.
- Sit and soak in the medicine you've created.

4

Green

Green is the color of a natural healing energy. It comes with all of the light and the shadow of what the energy of healing exudes.

To keep your green in balance, make sure you are following your heart. In relationships especially, yours is a heart that wants to give, so be sure you aren't surrounding yourself with people who solely want to take. Sometimes it is important to speak up when you feel someone you love is causing harm. Sometimes it is important to trust their process when they do things you disagree with. If you can stay present in your own body, your heart will always tell you where you should go, what you should do, and how you need to get there.

Be careful of overvaluing others' opinions of you. Even if they mean well, the opinion that comes from outside of you holds nothing against the strength of your own heart. Trust that wisdom and you will find yourself exactly where you need to be.

THE LIGHT

Green is a color of healing. A color of positive growth and creativity, though not necessarily artistic. Green is a lover. Compassionate, empathetic, nurturing, creative, connected to nature, a mother to children, plants, animals, and others.

THE SHADOW

The shadow side of green in the aura is internalizing someone else's process and making it your own. Because it is so easy to for you to sense what others are feeling, you can sometimes end up literally embodying their emotions. Greens think too much about what others need to do in order to make things easier for themselves; they're too involved in the lives of others. They often have difficulty being present with their own situations. Greens at their most shadowy can have a tendency toward gossip.

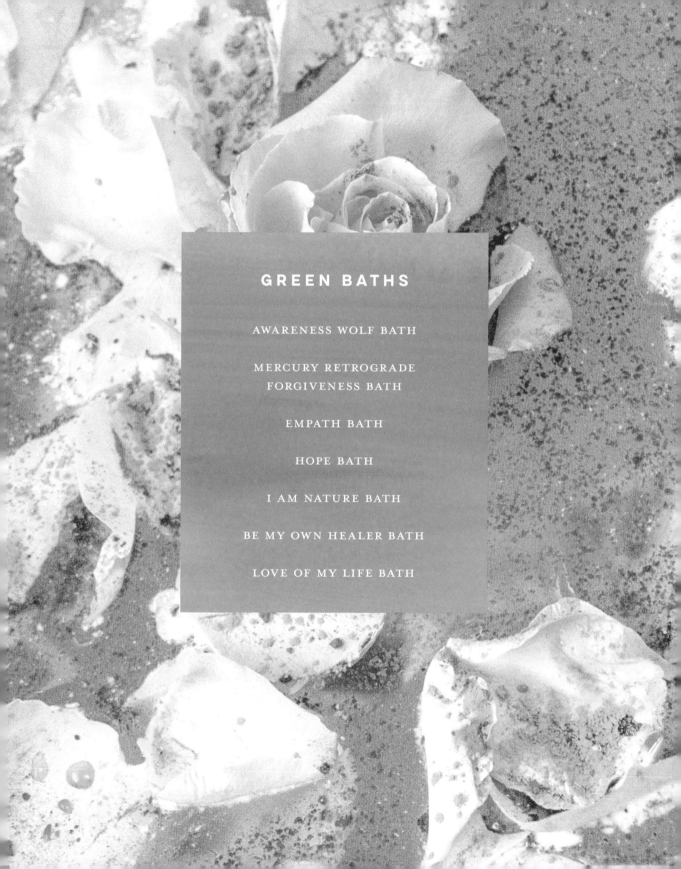

GREEN BATHS

AWARENESS WOLF BATH

MERCURY RETROGRADE
FORGIVENESS BATH

EMPATH BATH

HOPE BATH

I AM NATURE BATH

BE MY OWN HEALER BATH

LOVE OF MY LIFE BATH

Awareness Wolf Bath

NORTH, EARTH, WINTER, CAPRICORN, AQUARIUS
TEA PAIRING: LEMON BALM, ROSE, AND BASIL TEA

I woke up one morning while the moon was still in the sky. I stared at her with a deep gratitude emanating in my heart for my ancestors, and the incredible experiences they went through in order for me to be here today. I felt a rush of wisdom about the patterns I carry from them, and how to work with these behaviors and grow from them. An understanding that is as old as life itself: When we are present and aware we are protected. Just as a mother wolf nourishes her cubs and simultaneously is tuned into everything in her surroundings. This bath is a reverence for intuition. Here is to the beginning of something new by remembering things that have passed.

Ingredients

2 cups pink Himalayan salt

A pot of lemon balm tea

A dash of rosewater

1 cup dragon fruit powder

1 cup coconut milk

1 cup wild rose, also known as wolf rose
(Rosa acicularis), fresh or dried

1 cup fresh basil leaves

1 cup frozen berries

10 drops each of sweet orange and patchouli essential oils

Rose quartz crystal

Ritual

- Place all the ingredients in the bath at a temperature of your choosing.
- With your intention in your heart, light a candle.
- Step into the bath.
- Place the rose quartz crystal anywhere on your body.
- Be present. Soak in the energy of the smells, colors, and sounds of your bath. Soak in the energy of awareness.
- When you finish bathing, blow out the candle. Offer all the plants used to the earth in gratitude.

Mercury Retrograde Forgiveness Bath

EAST, WIND, AUTUMN, SAGITTARIUS
TEA PAIRING: NETTLE, LEMON BALM, AND OAT STRAW TEA

Mercury Retrograde has gotten a really bad rap for being the crusher of plans and expectations. However, if we try going with the flow of Mercury Retrograde, it can be a very helpful time for illuminating our patterns and cycles that are no longer in our highest interest.

Mercury Retrograde starts kicking our butts when we try to make plans to escape. This can be through traveling, by starting a new project, or by focusing on our electronics in order to avoid looking at the habits that are being revealed to us.

Instead of trying to push forward, this is an amazing time to let yourself float through life. Tie up loose ends you are dealing with and settle into the present moment. This is a wonderful time for reflection and journaling. It is a time for looking deep within ourselves to reveal hidden answers to our biggest questions.

Mercury Retrograde can bring up very uncomfortable waves of anxiety and depression in even the most balanced among us. It is important that we allow ourselves to feel these feelings, for sometimes it is through discomfort that lessons are revealed to us. Mercury Retrograde acts as a reminder of how to forgive past wounding and hurt. We start to understand that as long as we hold grudges, as long as we are still angry, we will continue to let ourselves be wounded. In fact, we are the ones hurting ourselves. In the end, isn't it always ourselves we need to forgive?

We put ourselves in the circumstances we need in order to grow. If you are past the age of seventeen and still haven't forgiven your parents for how you grew up, consider that maybe your wise, wise spirit chose your parents because they were the people who would give you the upbringing that would teach you the lessons you need to learn in this lifetime. By being grateful for your wisdom gained, you can forgive almost anything. Anger, hatred, and intolerance will always bring you more suffering. Understanding leads to forgiveness, forgiveness leads to compassion, and compassion leads to love.

This bath is designed to help us find acceptance for all that is being revealed to us.

Ingredients

A pot of nettle tea

10 drops of sweet orange and 5 drops of
cedarwood essential oils

A handful of ivy leaves

Labradorite crystal

Ritual

- Place all the ingredients in the bath at a temperature of your choosing.
- Cover yourself in some kind of earth (I recommend a bentonite clay body mask).
- Create a smudge using white sage by putting it in a nonflammable tray of some kind and igniting it. Waft the smoke around your body using a feather you have found.
- Step into the bath and dunk your head underwater.
- Place the labradorite crystal on your heart center.
- Close your eyes.
- In your mind's eye, run through all the people in your life whose actions have hurt you. Who are you ready to forgive? Try to understand where they are coming from and why they've hurt you. Have compassion for them. Think about what you learned from them. Thank them for all they have taught you, and then let them go into love. Forgive them. Forgive yourself for needing to experience so much pain in order to learn these lessons.
- Breathe deeply and invite in any revelations you are needing at this time.
- Sit and soak in the medicine of forgiveness that you've created.

Empath Bath

WATER, WEST, SPRING, CANCER, AQUARIUS
TEA PAIRING: JASMINE, LINDEN, AND ROSE TEA

If Greens are anything, they are compassionate. Their capacity for empathy and seeing things from others' points of view is uncanny. In extreme cases, this ability can be debilitating for them to the point where they feel they need to isolate themselves from others and the intrusion of their energy. But people with extreme empathy need to be very, very brave. Why? Because the world needs you, maybe now more than ever. People who feel all the feels, we need your voice, so we can see things through your perspective. You and your immense capacity for empathy and compassion are here to guide us all into unity consciousness. You are here to remind us of how everything we do, say, and think affects the collective consciousness. Why do you think you are so sensitive? Do you really think that this powerful gift is here to weaken you and keep you tucked away?

What if empathy turned into generosity and you began to share all that you see and feel? Even sharing with just one person could potentially inspire them to share what they learned from you. The compassion you have could grow and grow.

This is why I try not to get upset when people directly copy me. Sometimes people copy the brand, the words I use, or act like they just came up with the idea for the Ritual Bath they are sharing. I don't mind if what they are sharing always links back to love. I'm not here to take the credit for it, I'm here to share and spread love. If you are reading this, I have a feeling you are too, so let's get to work!

This bath is designed to help you feel that much more empathic.

Ingredients

1 cup pink Himalayan sea salt

3 tablespoons blue-green algae

1 cup coconut milk

Fresh pink roses

3 drops each of gardenia and jasmine
essential oils

Rose quartz and emerald crystals

Ritual

- Place all the ingredients in the bath at a temperature of your choosing.
- Light a candle.
- Create a smudge using sweetgrass by putting it in a nonflammable tray of some kind and igniting it. Waft the smoke around your body using a feather you have found.
- Step into the bath and dunk your head underwater.
- Place the rose quartz crystal on your heart.
- Place your healing hands over the crystal.
- Invite your powerful heart to feel everything it wants to feel. Cry if you need to. This is your spirit's way of cleansing itself.
- Invite this holy temple that you carry with you wherever you go to guide you and teach you.
- Sit and soak in the power of love you've created.

Hope Bath

WATER, EAST, SPRING, PISCES, LIBRA, GEMINI
TEA PAIRING: DANDELION, NETTLE, AND VIOLET LEAF AND FLOWER TEA

When I was seventeen I got very, very deep into Zen meditation. I'd wake up at four every morning to count my breaths, walk, and meditate. I felt so much peace in the nothingness and simplicity of it. Part of the philosophy of Zen is having no expectations. I deeply understood that. If we don't have expectations, then we cannot be disappointed. How very freeing that notion felt to me. Later, I would connect that this idea held such comfort for me because it came at the time that my parents were going through their very messy divorce and told me I needed to figure out my own place to live.

Around that same time, the Metropolitan Museum of Art was holding a William Blake exhibit. I was spellbound by his paintings and words. He wrote, "Hope is banished from me." I remember feeling struck by how this artist put into words the exact way I felt. My dad had just replaced our family with his new one and hated tattoos, so being a rebellious Scorpio, I got that very quote tattooed across my back.

What I didn't understand is that hope and expectation are two very, very different things. Expectation can lead to disappointment, but sometimes all you have is hope. As a result of living on my own at such a young age, hope was a constant feeling. I would hope that a stranger would be kind enough to give me money to buy a MetroCard so I could get to an interview for a job that I hoped I would be hired for. I would hope a friend would see how hungry I was and offer to make me a meal. I would hope that one day my dad would be my dad again. I hoped all the time, but I didn't expect anything. When the things I had hoped for happened, I was pleasantly surprised.

If I look back on the exact time that I got that tattoo on my back, I can see that hope was getting me through that hard time in my life. After having those words on my back for a couple of years, I realized they did not feel like me anymore. I was ready for all the gifts life had to bring me. Free of expectation, but full of hope. I got the tattoo covered up with another tattoo of wind, a representation of transformation.

And guess what? My dad did end up coming back around. When my daughter was born, he started showing up as a wonderful grandfather, and I have a good enough relationship with both of my parents now. I see them as people, doing what they need to do to grow. I let go of the expectation that when you are a parent you need to have it all figured out, because that idea always led me to disappointment. I'm grateful for those difficult times because they made me who I am today.

If you feel lost, like you've been cast aside, and full of despair, know you are not alone. You are a very important part of this collective consciousness. Without you, something would be missing. Yes, you may be experiencing great loss, but if you seek it out, there is always hope. If you cannot find hope, watch nature. At the very end of the long silence of winter, the Earth and all of her creatures are so full of the hope that spring will soon return, that the sun will smile again, that soon everything will start to sing. You too will shine on, and you too will sing again. This bath can remind you that no matter how dark the night may be, the light will always return. Infuse the color green, a color of healing and hope, into your aura. Let this bath rejuvenate you.

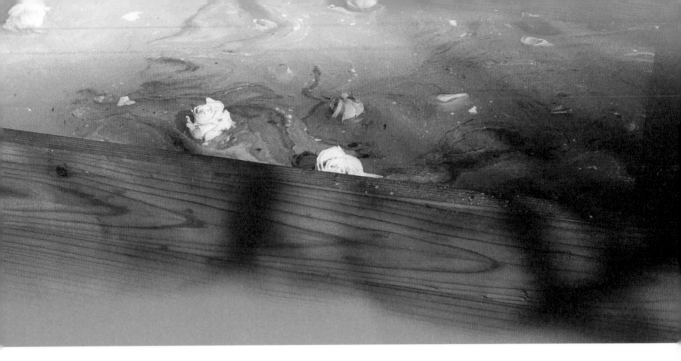

Ingredients

1 cup pink Himalayan sea salt

1 cup hemp milk

1 cup green juice (ideally with dandelion greens)

A pot of nettle tea

Olive branches and leaves

4 drops of cedarwood and 10 drops of rose absolute essential oils, mixed into 3 tablespoons honey

Rose quartz crystal

Jade crystal

Ritual

- Place all the ingredients in the bath at a temperature of your choosing.
- Light a candle.
- Create a smudge using dried cedar by putting it in a nonflammable tray of some kind and igniting it. Waft the smoke around your body using a feather you have found.
- Step into the bath and dunk your head underwater.
- Sing any song that comforts you.
- Let the singing cleanse your soul.
- Let the water hold and support you.
- Let the crystals remind you how much the earth loves you.
- Soak in the medicine you've created.

I Am Nature Bath

EARTH, NORTH, SUMMER, TAURUS
TEA PAIRING: NETTLE, RED CLOVER, ROSE, AND DANDELION TEA

Even if they live in the middle of a big city, people who have a green aura will always find a way to stay connected to nature. Because they are filled with so much empathy, they often need to escape into nature to ground and let the soft winds, water, and earth cleanse their spirits. Even a simple house plant on a windowsill of your midtown walk-up can remind you what you know to be inherently true: You are nature! The earth is your body, the wind is your breath, the water is your blood, and the fire is your spirit. The reason you may connect to crystals is because they speak to the minerals in your body and remind you that you, too, are a part of this beautiful Earth. We take care of our bodies the same way we take care of the Earth. When you are going through a phase of eating unhealthfully and skipping workouts, watch and see if you are also buying more plastic and engaging in other practices that harm the Earth. The more we can realize that we are nature, the more we can take care of her.

When we talk about getting grounded, what we are really talking about is returning to the source, returning to the truth of where we come from, returning to the earth. This bath is designed to help us to remember the truth of who we are. Follow this bath with a walk outside.

Ingredients

Red clay, mixed with bentonite clay and graviola powder, nettle leaf powder, or matcha

1 cup black lava salt

1 cup pink rose petals

1 bunch of fresh rosemary

10 drops each of rose and rosemary essential oils

All of your non-water-soluble crystals

Ritual

- Mix clay and plant powders with spring water to create a thick paste.
- Cover your body head to toe with the mixture.
- If you have the luxury, go outside naked, covered in the mixture. Stand in the sun. When the paste begins to dry, rub it off your body. It will create a fine, very exfoliating dust. Notice how grounding and awakening this practice is.
- If you cannot go outside naked and covered in green mud because your neighbors will be convinced that the zombie apocalypse is here, then prepare your bath while you're letting the mixture dry.
- Place all the other ingredients in the bath at a temperature of your choosing.
- Light a candle.
- Create a smudge using white sage by putting it in a nonflammable tray of some kind and igniting it. Waft the smoke around your body using a feather you have found.
- Step into the bath and dunk your head underwater.
- Place the crystals on your body wherever your intuition is guided to place them.
- Sing this song (original author unknown):

Earth my body.
Water my blood.
Wind my breath.
And fire my spirit.

- Take ten deep, grounding breaths.
- Sit and soak in the medicine you've created.

Be My Own Healer Bath

ALL DIRECTIONS, ALL ELEMENTS, ALL SEASONS, ALL SIGNS
TEA PAIRING: LEMON BALM, SELF-HEAL, NETTLE, LINDEN,
AND GOLDENROD TEA

*Kindness is more important than wisdom, and the
recognition of this is the beginning of wisdom.*
—THEODORE ISAAC RUBIN

Green people tend to have an ease of connecting to their own healing energy. Call this color into your aura when you are seeking clarity on how you can best be your own healer. We are all healers, because we all have the power of love within us. Think about how you feel when you are with an animal you love, or tending to one of your beautiful plants. That feeling is the power of love.

We have to be so careful to not give our power away to other false healers. You don't need to be fixed, because you are not broken. When you go to see a healer, remember that they can share only what they see from their perspective; you always have to process whatever anyone else says through your own powerful intuition. Don't trust that someone else knows better than you just because they wear the right outfit and say deep things. And if you do go see someone else for your healing, the first thing you should be looking for is if they are loving and kind. How do they treat the people around them? Because the sign of a true healer is not what someone says, wears, eats, or drinks, but if they take the many opportunities on any given day to be kind. If you want to be a healer to others, set an example of self-healing. Have the courage to follow your own wisdom, even if you're afraid of being judged by others. That will inspire others to heal themselves. Set an example of kindness and love. You have so much wisdom. Trust that wise heart of yours and you will, with time and patience, know what it is you need to do to heal yourself.

If you don't know where to begin with being your own healer, start with being kind to yourself. Take yourself outside and into nature as much as possible, especially if you are feeling down or overwhelmed. Let fresh air and the feeling of the sun on your skin and earth under your feet heal you. The next step is not being afraid to objectively reflect on your past experiences. Chances are, you've already been through things that can help you to understand why you are where you are in this moment. There is wisdom to be had in everything, and from this wisdom, you can choose to grow. Let yourself be inspired by nature, inspired by your inner child, inspired by the world around you. Do little things to stimulate your creativity again, like making a dinner for yourself that you've never made before.

This bath can help you come into the power of being your own healer. You don't need to have any attunements, certifications, or degrees to heal. You need only feel the power of love within you.

Ingredients

1 cup pink Himalayan sea salt

1 tablespoon blue-green algae

A tub tea of lemon balm, self-heal, nettle, linden, and goldenrod

1 cup pumpkin seed milk

Pink rose petals

Pink chrysanthemums

Rose quartz and clear quartz crystals

Ritual

- Place all the ingredients in the bath at a temperature of your choosing.
- Light a candle.
- Create a smudge using white sage by putting it in a nonflammable tray of some kind and igniting it. Waft the smoke around your body using a feather you have found.
- Step into the bath and dunk your head underwater.
- Connect to the energy in your heart. Imagine a green golden light emanating from it. This light carries the power of love. Imagine this light from your heart traveling down all throughout your body and then moving down your arms into your hands.
- Feel your hands pulsing with the power of love. Let them guide you from your intuition to where they want to be placed.
- Continue to let your hands travel to different positions around your body as you let the power of love within yourself heal you.
- Sit and soak in the magic and medicine you've created.

Love of My Life Bath

WATER, SOUTH, AUTUMN, SCORPIO
TEA PAIRING: PASSION FRUIT, ROSE HIP, VIOLET,
WILD ROSE, AND HAWTHORN BERRY TEA

Green is the color to work with when you are calling in the love of your life. This is because green is a color of healing and growth, and if you let it, love will heal you. It will also hurt you, challenge you, and make you uncomfortable, because sometimes this is what we humans need in order to grow. When you are calling in the love of your life, call in the power of love. Here again I will mention to be a bit careful with telling the universe exactly what you want. Be open. True love doesn't always appear in the package we think it should. The love of your life may not have the career you want them to have or the looks you were expecting, but they may be the person who will love you deeper and more truly than you could ever imagine.

A few months after I went through a terrible breakup, my friends had a couch that they wanted to give me. When they came to drop it off, they had a friend of theirs (and also the most handsome guy I'd ever seen) helping them. When he sat down on the couch and started talking to me, I felt so nervous that I couldn't even look at him. When they left, a knowing friend checked to see if I could tell that the hot guy had been flirting with me. I was in shock. Wait, he was . . . flirting? With . . . me?

A few days later, after an ayahuasca ceremony I invited him to, he wrote me a poem, with pen and beautiful paper; it was eight pages long, containing details in it no one could've ever known about me. I was out of town at a friend's wedding, so he read it to me over the phone and then left it in my mailbox. I got home to discover it had a picture of a girl peacefully resting with a lion protecting her. Three days later he took me on our first date. He sat next to me in a booth at a Vietnamese restaurant, turned to me, and told me that he would never be with anyone else in his life, that he was going to marry me one day, and that he'd wait for me for as long as I needed. That sounded good to me.

After only four days of being together, before even sleeping together, being the impulsive Scorpio that I am, I asked him to move in with me.

He spent the next eight months proving how much he loved me. When I was away for a weekend, he redesigned and furnished my entire apartment, exactly how I had explained to him that I wanted it. He painted my whole yoga studio/healing center, and he rented me a parking space for my car (which in NYC is one of the most romantic things someone can do).

He took me to stay in castles in his country, the Netherlands. He took me shopping in Paris, followed by dinner at a Michelin-starred restaurant at the top of the Eiffel Tower. No matter what city we were in or what we were doing, we would have to stop by benches, bridges, and cafés just to stare at each other. Like we couldn't believe we found each other again in this lifetime.

After those eight months, we became pregnant with our daughter, which was (at that point) the happiest day of our lives. I had to close my yoga studio and healing center because I was having a hard time getting the numbers back to where they had been before my ex spread some vicious rumors, and because coming into my truth also meant that working twelve-hour days, seven days a week just wasn't good for me and impossible to do while pregnant. Closing my business was like the death of someone I loved. And throughout that hard time, I was supported, emotionally and financially, by this man who just wanted to love and take care of me.

When you are calling in the love of your life, make sure you are not doing anything to specifically block that person from coming to you. Do you often develop feelings for people who don't live in the same area as you? Check to make sure that you aren't going for people who are unavailable because you are trying to protect yourself from falling in love and possibly getting hurt. Do you have someone in your life that you keep around so that you don't feel lonely? This person could be acting as a locked door to your calling in the love of your life. Risk being lonely; get to know and love yourself by being alone with yourself. That will help you find someone who knows and loves themselves, which will lead you to a healthy relationship. Have you had no relationship for a very long time?

Check to see if you can really trust people, check to see if you trust yourself. Do you feel like you are always meeting the wrong people? What is the common thread that connects all of them? Check to see if that energy is somewhere in you. The reason you keep meeting people with the same kind of hang-ups could be because you are being shown the things that you yourself need to work on.

Do words like *twin flame* and *soul mate* put too much pressure on a relationship? I think so. It is already hard enough to truly open up and allow others in. When we are immediately searching for signs that they are our twin flame, we are putting expectation into a brand-new relationship. Yes, you may have been together lifetime upon lifetime, but you are meeting again in this one to discover something new. Let the relationship be new and let it be a deep and wonderful connection.

Of course it comes back to this: If we want someone else to love us truly, we first must love ourselves. Once we do this, we will radiate the energy of love. This bath is designed to open the door to true love.

Ingredients

2 tablespoons dragon fruit powder

A tub tea of passion fruit, rose hips, violet, wild rose, and hawthorn berries

1 cup coconut milk

1 cup strawberry juice

Pink, red, and white rose petals

Leaves from 1 bunch of fresh basil

Eucalyptus leaves

10 drops of rose absolute, 5 drops of linden, and 5 drops of frankincense essential oils mixed into 2 tablespoons honey

Rose quartz crystal

Clear quartz crystal

The Dream: Fresh violet leaves

Ritual

- Place all the ingredients in the bath at a temperature of your choosing.
- Light a candle.
- Create a smudge using palo santo by putting it in a nonflammable tray of some kind and igniting it. Waft the smoke around your body using a feather you have found.
- Cleanse your aura with a selenite wand.
- Step into the bath and dunk your head underwater.

- Ask the water to show you what it is that you may be doing that could possibly block you from meeting the love of your life.
- Ask the water to teach you patience and trust that this person will come in at the right moment for you and not before or after.
- Hold the rose quartz crystal and ask the crystal to teach you the power of self-love.
- Hold the clear quartz crystal and ask the crystal to teach you the power of trust, of trusting love, life, and yourself.
- Sit and soak in the magic and medicine you've created.

5

Blue

Blue in the aura is a color with multiple meanings. Every different shade of blue has its own nuances. For example, turquoise in the aura represents the trust that comes from the confidence of knowing oneself. A sky blue indicates a very open and friendly person. A cobalt blue shows a deep connection to spirit and one who can feel or communicate with spirits. Indigo is a blue with so much to it, it needs its own section. As open as Blues are, blue in the aura can also mean feeling the blues. Since Blues are very honest, they can feel depressed if they are not living their truth.

THE LIGHT

Blues are the best communicators because they are great listeners. They are genuinely curious about others. They are so open-minded that they will try just about anything once. They have their own approach to spirituality. Even if they are raised in a certain religion, they have their own way of interpreting all they hear and experience. No matter what anyone says to them, Blues will turn to their own truth before believing anything.

THE SHADOW

Being so committed to what is true, Blue people can often be suspicious of others and can come off as overly righteous if they aren't careful. Even though they are open-minded, they can still be pretty judgmental and have fixed ideas of right and wrong. Depression is the biggest part of the shadow with Blues.

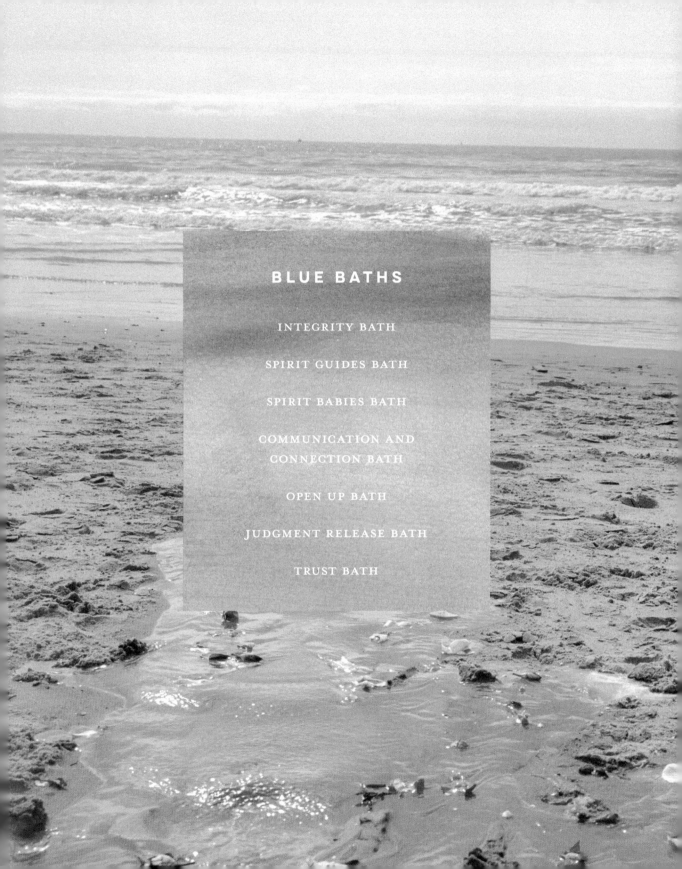

BLUE BATHS

INTEGRITY BATH

SPIRIT GUIDES BATH

SPIRIT BABIES BATH

COMMUNICATION AND
CONNECTION BATH

OPEN UP BATH

JUDGMENT RELEASE BATH

TRUST BATH

Integrity Bath

EAST, WIND, SPRING, SCORPIO, CANCER, LEO
TEA PAIRING: LEMON BALM, LEMONGRASS, ELDERBERRY,
AND SLIPPERY ELM TEA

Call the color blue into your aura when you have the feeling that you may be having a hard time being honest with yourself. So resistant to change are we that we can often keep ourselves in situations that have long since served their purpose. To be honest with ourselves about how we are feeling may bring about change, and change brings pain, so we go about our day avoiding the truth and hoping it won't scream at us too loudly. *Spiritual bypassing* is a term for when we use spiritual excuses like "the moon made me do it." Instead of hiding from or avoiding the things we feel, let's consciously confront ourselves or those close to us so that we can grow.

In my twenties, I was in a long-term relationship with someone who in so many ways didn't know himself. He did not even know his name. In that relationship, I was more the mom than the partner. I was both emotionally and financially supporting him by working twelve-hour days, seven days a week at my yoga studio. I'd come home to a filthy house reeking of beer and weed and dogs who desperately needed to be walked. I knew that this relationship was unhealthy, but I didn't want to hurt him, so I just spiritually bypassed and focused on the good in the relationship—I was living a lie. Toward the end, I couldn't be around him anymore without clenching my jaw.

One day the words *I'm done* just fell out of my mouth. I couldn't possibly hold the truth in any longer. I told him he needed to go figure out who he was, and that the relationship was holding us both back. I told him I needed to be in a relationship with someone who is proud of who he is and doesn't use substances to repress himself. When he moved out, he took *everything*. All of my furniture, my clothes—everything. And I let him because I felt bad that he was now going to have to take care of himself. He tried to take me down and ruin my business by telling all of my friends, neighbors, and clients that I had left him for someone else, because he was worried I would tell people the real reason we were splitting up. I didn't let myself hate him for doing that—I knew how scared he

was. Instead, I figured the truth would set me free. People would see that I wasn't with someone else, and they could believe what they wanted.

Speaking my truth and freeing myself from that first toxic relationship led me to the happiest time in my life. I married the handsome man and allowed myself to be truly loved. With that energy, I gave birth to my daughter and rebuilt my healing practice. The truth didn't only set me free, it gave me wings to fly.

If you are feeling stuck or blocked in life, check to see if you are really in alignment with your truth. This bath is designed to give you some time to check in and take heed of what is true for you.

Ingredients

1 cup Epsom salt

A tub tea of lemon balm, mullein, elderberry, and slippery elm

5 drops of lemongrass and 10 drops of lavender essential oils mixed into 1 cup coconut milk

2 tablespoons Blue Majik powder

White rose petals, cornflowers, blue hydrangeas, violets

Turquoise, blue apatite, and larimar polished crystals

The Dream: Forget-me-nots

Ritual

- Place all the ingredients in the bath at a temperature of your choosing.
- Light a candle.
- Create a smudge using palo santo by putting it in a nonflammable tray of some kind and igniting it. Waft the smoke around your body using a feather you have found.
- Step into the bath and dunk your head underwater.
- Place your crystals on your heart, upper belly, and right below the belly button.
- Close your eyes.
- Ask the water to remind you who you are.
- Ask the water to give you the courage to know your truth.
- Soak in the medicine you've created.

Spirit Guides Bath

EAST, EARTH, AUTUMN, ALL SIGNS
TEA PAIRING: WHITE PINE AND WILD ROSE TEA

Spirit guides are energies of plants, animals, stars, ancestors, angels, and multidimensional beings who guide and protect us. From my perspective, everyone has spirit guides and sometimes they show up in Medicine Readings with messages for my clients. In the ceremony part of a Medicine Reading, they come through to pour their love, healing, and medicine on my clients. Actually, during the ceremony, I feel like it isn't even me doing any of the work. I feel like more of a recipient than anything. The client's guides come through, happily getting the chance to work with them.

When I look at someone's aura, spirit guides are almost always cobalt blue dots. Depending on where in the aura they are, I can see if it is an ancestor, an angel, an animal, or something else.

One of the superpowers of being your own healer is even without a Medicine Reading, you can meet your spirit guides. This simple kitchen witch Ritual Bath can help.

Ingredients

1 cup salt (any kind)

At least 1 cup fresh or dried rosemary (if dried, make a tub tea)

½ cup fresh or dried thyme (if dried, make a tub tea)

½ cup fresh or dried basil (if dried, make a tub tea)

1 cup blackberries and blueberries mixed in with 3 cups milk, 1 tablespoon honey, and 1 tablespoon vanilla extract

10 drops of lavender essential oil

Moon water (to make, set a cup of clean water on a windowsill during a full moon to catch the light)

Any non-water-soluble crystals you have (ideally ones you found yourself in nature)

1 fresh cucumber, sliced

Ritual

- Add each ingredient to the running water of your bath as an offering to your guides.
- Light a candle.

- Create a smudge using a cinnamon stick by putting it in a nonflammable tray of some kind and igniting it. Waft the smoke around your body using a feather you have found.
- Step into the bath and dunk your head underwater.
- Place the palms of your hands on the surface of the water.
- Close your eyes and go into a meditation.
- Go to that special place within yourself where no one else can go.
- Invite your spirit guides one at a time to come meet you there.
- Introduce yourself to them and ask them questions, like you are meeting a new friend.
- Thank them for all they do for you.
- Be patient, you guides may come through in the bath or they may come later in your dreams or waking visions.
- Take time after the bath or after meeting your guides to journal characteristics about them or things that they told you.

Spirit Babies Bath

WEST, WATER, SPRING, GEMINI
TEA PAIRING: RED CLOVER, ROSE HIP,
RED RASPBERRY LEAF, AND NETTLE TEA

When people come to see me for Medicine Readings, I sometimes see the children they are yet to have, adoptive children, children who are working with them on the spiritual plane as guides, and sadly children that they have had, or almost had, but have lost. I see this whether the person is asking me about children or not. When a client isn't specifically asking me about having a baby, I use my discernment and reveal very little. But sometimes the spirit of the child who wants to come through for them is so loud that I have to say something. I see if they are in a place in their lives where they aren't ready to hear it, and I proceed from there.

The spirits of babies yet to come through are often guiding their parents to the life choices that are needed for conception to occur. I'm not surprised, for example, when a client comes in saying she is feeling stuck, thinks she may need to quit her job, and also has a spirit baby right next to her head. That soul is just waiting for the right moment to come through. Because this process of unblocking ourselves can be so extensive, and things like trying to conceive can take so long, I see people get discouraged and feel like they are doing something wrong. But I think that is just the spirit of the child trying to teach their future parent patience.

Spirit children can sometimes be our ancestors coming back to us to have another chance to grow together. It is totally case by case, but when a client has a miscarriage, I feel like this is the spirit of the baby telling her that they are coming, so get ready! Or they want to come, but there is still one little thing that is off in the parents' energy that they want to see transform before they can come through fully. Of course, sometimes without spiritual explanation, miscarriages just happen.

To lose a child is an unimaginable heartbreak. When clients come in who have experienced a loss this great, I often see that the spirit of the child was an ancestor of theirs or someone they had unfinished business with in a past life. This is a footbath designed

to help you connect to your spirit child and ask them to guide you to what they need from you.

Ingredients

1 cup Epsom salt

A tub tea of chamomile tea

A rose quartz crystal

White rose petals

Orange peels

A few drops of lavender essential oil

Ritual

- Put all the ingredients into a footbath.
- Light a candle.
- Place your feet in the bath.
- Cleanse your aura with a selenite wand.
- Close your eyes.
- Go into a meditative state.
- Invite your spirit child to give you signs of anything you need to learn.
- Be open to those signs for a week after your footbath.
- Repeat this footbath once a week until you feel clear.

Communication and Connection Bath

FIRE, SOUTH, SUMMER, GEMINI, AQUARIUS, AIRES
TEA PAIRING: BUTTERFLY PEA FLOWER AND ELDERBERRY TEA

We have a tendency to stick to what and who we know. But could this be blocking us from connections that could truly help us grow? Blue is such a spiritual color. It is often the color that spirits will appear in. Could a fear of connection and communication keep us from connecting to our guides and guardians who are here to help us?

Blues are great communicators and have an easy time being open to new people they meet. Blue people can often even communicate with spirits. They are often natural mediums. If you have the energy of mediumship, meaning you can channel messages from spirits, this is a gift to be used for good. Use it to help spirits transition; use it to relay important messages from the great mystery. Try not to be afraid of the spirits who come to you.

When people die and they don't know that they are dead, which is sometimes the case with overdose, murder, and suicide, they remain somewhere in between the third dimension and the great mystery until they understand that they have died. They either stay in the place where they died or they follow loved ones around. These are ghosts. I get asked a lot about what people should do about ghosts in their homes or around them. A lot of times people get scared and they try to forcefully extract the ghost, demanding that it leave. But I don't think this helps; I think it just confuses ghosts, since they believe they are still alive. The ghosts are like, "Wait, why is this person asking me to leave my own house?" They then feel offended and start messing with the people, moving stuff around and waking them up in the middle of the night. Sometimes you move into a home where ghosts are already sinister. This can be because the person who lived there before you was mean to them or maybe they were just sinister people during their lives. Either way, if you want to deal with a ghost in your house or around you, be gentle.

Light some sage, open a window, and gently and compassionately let them know that they have died. Let them know it's time for them to transition into the great mystery. Tell them the sage will guide them. Lead them toward the open window and set them free.

Trust your very wise intuition to communicate with your guides, guardians, angels, and ancestors yourself through your emotional body. This is the power of Blues being so incredibly connected to their emotional bodies that it also connects them to their intuition. In a way we are all mediums at different necessary moments, able to channel works of art or beautiful meals or know how to say the right thing to someone who is grieving. Those you love and have lost will send you signs that only you can interpret—like a hawk flying in the sky or other things that deeply remind you of them. These signs are showing you they are okay, that they are in a good place and that they still love you.

The color blue, like the wide-open ocean, like the wide-open sky, is one of receptivity. It is a color of being able to see things from another's perspective, while maintaining your sense of self. Most of being a great communicator is being a great listener, taking a moment to digest what the other has said and where they are coming from. Blue is such a wonderful color to call into your aura when you want to know how to better communicate what is deep within you. When you are feeling brave enough to expose your wide-open self to the ideas of others, this bath can help.

Ingredients

1 cup Epsom salt

A tub tea of butterfly tea powder

Yellow rose petals

3 drops each of frankincense, lemon balm, and rose absolute essential oils mixed into 1 cup each of milk and honey

Turquoise crystal

Frankincense tears

Ritual

- Place all the ingredients in the bath at a temperature of your choosing.
- Light a candle.
- Cleanse your aura with a selenite wand.
- Step into the bath and dunk your head underwater.
- Call in the energy of the kingfisher bird and the blue morpho butterfly.
- Ask the animals, plants, stones, and water to help you clear your fear around communication.
- Sit and soak in the magic you've created.

Open Up Bath

WATER, WEST, AUTUMN, LIBRA
TEA PAIRING: BUTTERFLY PEA FLOWER, WILD ROSE FLOWER,
AND LEMONGRASS TEA

You were born with potential. You were born with goodness and trust.
You were born with ideals and dreams. You were born with greatness.
You were born with wings. You are not meant for crawling, so don't.
You have wings. Learn to use them and fly.

—RUMI

It can be so hard to avoid being poured into molds by both ourselves and others. What is even worse is that people are afraid of others who are free. That's why for hundreds of years, women who connected to their divine wildness were executed as witches. In the history of our spirits, there are many of us who carry the wounding of being hunted or made an outcast for being different from past lives. We now stay in our lanes, color inside the lines, and hide in our nice cozy box.

But is this the life that's truly meant for us?

When you can stay open to the idea that things don't always have to be one way, you can learn so much about the world you live in, about others, and about yourself. How can you ever know and trust yourself if you cannot open up and sing your song?

This bath is designed to help you step out of the box.

Ingredients

1 cup Epsom salt

A tub tea of butterfly pea flower, wild rose
    flower, and lemongrass

½ watermelon, sliced

Red rose petals

A sprinkle of gold mica powder

Rose quartz crystals

10 drops of rose absolute essential oil

The Dream: Grape leaves

Ritual

- Place all the ingredients in the bath at a temperature of your choosing.
- Light a candle.
- Create a smudge using palo santo by putting it in a nonflammable tray of some kind and igniting it. Waft the smoke around your body using a feather you have found.
- Step into the bath and dunk your head underwater.
- Take ten deep, cleansing breaths, releasing a sigh at the exhale.
- Scan your body, noticing where sensations differ. Try not to label those sensations as good, bad, right, or wrong.
- Let this practice drift you into meditation.
- Sit and soak in the wide-open energy you've created.

Judgment Release Bath

WATER, WEST, AUTUMN, AQUARIUS
TEA PAIRING: EUCALYPTUS TEA

We have all been bullies or bullied at some point in our lives. Actually, anytime we cast judgment on ourselves or another, we are being a bully. People use social media and reality TV to bully, and then there are those who righteously bully. At a time when we have so much collective shame to release, this can make a fear of being seen harder than ever. What if they misunderstand me? What if I say the wrong thing?

I want to point out that we pay too much attention to what people do on social media and to image, and maybe not enough attention to the people we are with and what they are saying. In person, if someone says something that we think is messed up, we can be brave and tell them. In person. This is how we can help each other grow. In person. Let's connect to our surroundings. Let's connect to the present. We can do a lot of growth together. In person.

Just because someone posts pictures of their cute cat every day doesn't mean that they aren't out there on the frontlines offering help to others. Maybe they just don't share that aspect of themselves publicly, but that doesn't mean their positive actions don't have a ripple effect.

A lot of people, despite the veil of social media, are doing their best, or at least trying to. Let's guide each other.

So, to the righteous bully, yes, you have your purpose and place, and I think you mean well, but just make sure you are going after the people who are truly causing harm. This is the moment we are beginning to let go of our judgments, compartmentalization, and assumptions about each other. When will we gain the wisdom of our collective shadow and truly learn how to love each other? Look beyond what the other believes, what he looks like, where he comes from, what he identifies with, wears, eats, or posts. Aren't we here to right the wrongs of our ancestors by absorbing, integrating, and applying the generational wisdom that this human family has gained? When will we learn to love each other?

We have to understand that as long as we are judging, we are causing harm, even

if that judgment is coming from a good place. Often we judge others because there is something within them that we see in ourselves. Call open-minded blue into your aura when you are having a hard time letting go of judgment of yourself or others. This bath is designed to help us to put our judgments in check.

Ingredients

5 cups Epsom salt

Fresh or dried eucalyptus

Pink rose petals

Polished celestite crystal

10 drops of rose absolute essential oil

Ritual

- Place all the ingredients in the bath at a temperature of your choosing.
- Light a candle.
- Step into the bath and dunk your head underwater.
- Place the celestite crystal on your heart.
- For a moment let yourself hear your judgmental mind, even speaking judgments you know you have out loud.
- Feel the vibration those words have created.
- Then ask the salt water to cleanse your spirit of the pain those judgments have caused.
- Dunk your head underwater again.
- Get out of the bath immediately.
- For the next few days after your bath, watch your inner dialog very closely. Notice how much you judge throughout your day. Try to put yourself in check and keep repeating this bath until you find this powerful moment: When you go to voice your judgments, you don't hear a thing.
- Then sit and soak in the medicine you've created.

Trust Bath

EARTH, WEST, WINTER, CAPRICORN
TEA PAIRING: ORANGE PEEL, ROSE PETAL, AND JASMINE TEA

To trust, we first must clear our judgment, our doubt, and our suspicions of ourselves and others. We clear the illusion of there being the other in the first place. Then, beyond our expectations, we find we are able to be open. We are able to receive the grace and abundance that have always been there, just waiting for us to open our palms, surrender, and say, "I am ready."

Trust the different sensations in your body and the feelings you have. This is intuition, and we all have it; the sensations and emotions we experience are the voice of our inner healer. Your inner healer is always with you in your wide-open heart, connecting you to your intuition through your emotions. The more you follow your intuition, the more it guides you. Listen to her. Trust yourself and your intuition and then you don't need to worry about whether others are trustworthy, because you know how you feel when you're around them. Instead of doubting yourself, have confidence in your own medicine. Be your own healer.

Ingredients

1 cup Epsom salt

2 tablespoons charcoal

2 tablespoons spirulina

1 cup milk (any kind)

3 oranges, sliced

1 cup pink rose petals

10 drops each of jasmine and
      sweet orange essential oils

Amethyst crystal

Ritual

- Place all the ingredients in the bath at a temperature of your choosing.
- Create a smudge using a cinnamon stick by putting it in a nonflammable tray of some kind and igniting it. Waft the smoke around your body using a feather you have found.
- Step into the bath and dunk your head underwater.

- Sing a song that helps you open into your body and the water.
- Take ten deep breaths.
- Sit and soak in the magic you've created.
- When you are done with the bath and the clean-up ritual, take time to rest with your legs up the wall for ten minutes. Notice how you feel.

6

Indigo

Indigo in the aura is one of my favorite colors to see. When a person with a lot of indigo comes in for a Medicine Reading, I have to be really mindful to not say anything as fact and simply just have a conversation with them and share energy together. Indigo folks are game changers. They are here to make the world a better place. They have an extremely hard time with outdated habits and patterns in our society. They are hyperaware of the fact that everything we say and do has an impact on the collective consciousness. They are heavily influenced by their many past lives.

THE LIGHT

People with a lot of indigo in their aura are natural teachers, even if they aren't choosing that particular profession. They teach through example. Because they are so averse to control, they never want to force others to do something. They are dreamers and change-makers. Trust is everything to Indigos. They will always keep your secrets. They will always show up on time. When they let people in, they let them in very deeply. You will almost never hear an Indigo engage in gossip about other people. They are allergic to lying. They live their truths no matter what it may cost them. They are the ones to go to when you need an honest opinion on something.

THE SHADOW

Most of the time, people with indigo in their aura have experienced a lot in their lifetime. This can make them seem older when they are still quite young. People have a tendency to read them the wrong way because of this. In any group situation, Indigos almost always have to be opposite. If everyone else is speaking or acting a certain way, they have to do it differently. This makes standard education and working for anyone else nearly impossible. Indigos sometimes feel misunderstood and, in truth, they often are. This can make them suspicious of others rather than trusting.

INDIGO BATHS

TRUTH BATH

DEEP LISTENING BATH

UNWOUNDED BATH

INTUITION BATH

WE ARE ALL CONNECTED BATH

SACRED REBEL BATH

Truth Bath

EARTH, NORTH, WINTER, CAPRICORN, LEO, SCORPIO, AQUARIUS
TEA PAIRING: LEMON BALM, ROSE, AND ASHWAGANDHA TEA

When you are searching for your truth, you need only look within to your own magnetic presence, the power of love that is constantly beating in your own wild heart. No one else, no tarot deck, seer, pendulum, or astrologer, can tell you where you should go or what you should do, because they don't have your magic. The quest for your purpose is one you must go on alone. But I can tell you this; you are here to give and receive love. The medium you use for this process is up to you, beloved wanderer. Bless your journey by taking this time to be your own healer.

Ingredients

1 cup pink Himalayan sea salt

A pot of lemon balm tea

A handful of pink rose petals

10 drops of jasmine essential oil

A turquoise or amazonite crystal

Any other non-water-soluble crystals

Ritual

- Place all the ingredients in the bath at a temperature of your choosing.
- Light a candle.
- Cleanse your aura with a selenite wand.
- Create a smudge using palo santo by putting it in a nonflammable tray of some kind and igniting it. Waft the smoke around your body using a feather you have found.
- Hold the turquoise or amazonite crystal in your left hand and place any other crystal allies around you in the water.
- Begin breathing at your own pace, taking two inhales through the nose and one exhale out of the mouth and finding your own rhythm.
- Tap into your own rhythm, your own heart, your own truth.
- Soak in the energy you've created.

Deep Listening Bath

WIND, EAST, WINTER, GEMINI, CANCER, LIBRA
TEA PAIRING: ROSE, NETTLE, AND LINDEN BLOSSOM TEA

This bath will soak in the energy of the east to evoke the power of listening. Deep listening enables many locked doors to open. The wind energy of the east will open your heart to what the surroundings of nature have to teach you. We are all being guided by the power of the great mystery.

When you need help to speak up, nature will support you. When you need to feel healed and cared for, she will support you. Take this bath when you feel the need to release external noise, to be quieter within, and call upon the sound of your inner voice. Give yourself ample time for this bath.

Ingredients

1 cup pink Himalayan sea salt

1 cup coconut milk

A handful of white rose petals

A pinch of activated charcoal

Labradorite crystal

Ritual

- Place all the ingredients in the bath at a temperature of your choosing.
- Light a candle.
- Create a smudge using white sage by putting it in a nonflammable tray of some kind and igniting it. Waft the smoke around your body using a feather you have found.
- Step into the bath and dunk your head underwater.
- Place the labradorite crystal on the place between your throat and your heart.
- Close your eyes.
- Begin to hum very softly and very lightly. Move the sound all around your throat, all around your heart, up into your head, and back down to your heart.
- Take this time to soak in the power of your truth.

Unwounded Bath

WATER, WEST, AUTUMN, SCORPIO
TEA PAIRING: BERGAMOT, NETTLE, ROSE, CALENDULA,
BORAGE, AND HEAL-ALL TEA

Yes, we carry our scars like memories, building and weaving the story of lifetimes into the fabric of our spirits. If we let them, our scars will give us wisdom. They will teach us about the mistakes we need not repeat, the ways we can become that much more aware. If we let our egos run loose with it, our scars can make it hard for us to trust others, or even hard for us to trust life, making us overly guarded and suspicious, and at worst paranoid and too afraid to let anyone or anything new into our lives. But we can let the wound heal. We can move forward. This bath is designed to help you do just that.

Ingredients

1 cup Epsom salt

A tub tea of endive and Earl Grey tea

2 tablespoons honey

Dandelion flowers and mugwort leaves

Smoky quartz crystals

The Dream: Comfrey honey with lemon balm essential oil

The Dream: Tub tea of heal-all, yarrow, borage, chicory, and calendula

The Dream: Marigold, lilac, and forget-me-not flowers

The Dream: Persian blue salt

Ritual

- Place all the ingredients in the bath at a temperature of your choosing.
- Create a smudge using mugwort by putting it in a nonflammable tray of some kind and igniting it. Waft the smoke around your body using a feather you have found.
- Take a deep breath and invite your inner elder, your inner wisdom, to come forth.
- Step into the bath and dunk your head underwater.
- If you have physical scars, take time to massage them gently with your smoky quartz crystals. As you do this, allow yourself to be open to any bits of wisdom and truth that might want to come forward for you from that scar. This is part of the story you carry.
- Sit and soak in the magic and medicine you've created.

Intuition Bath

WATER, WEST, AUTUMN, CANCER
TEA PAIRING: NETTLE AND DANDELION ROOT TEA

One place Indigos don't waver is the ability to listen to their intuition. Though they may not label it as such, they are always the ones who wake up out of a deep sleep after having a strong feeling about something. They are the ones making massive changes in their lives because of their feelings. From the outside, they are often viewed as impulsive, but they don't really care; they are not here to please people and to fit in. They are here to move shit. If you are having a hard time listening to your intuition or finding it in the first place, then infusing your aura with the energy of the Indigo can really help.

Ingredients

1 cup sea salt

A tub tea of mugwort, sage, green tea, thyme, and parsley

Bay leaf

1 fennel bulb, chopped

3 drops of patchouli and 10 drops of lemon balm essential oils

Lapis lazuli crystal

Ritual

- Place all the ingredients in the bath at a temperature of your choosing.
- Create a smudge using mugwort by putting it in a nonflammable tray of some kind and igniting it. Waft the smoke around your body using a feather you have found.
- Step into the bath and dunk your head underwater.
- Take ten deep breaths with your eyes closed and looking down into your heart.
- Get quiet—no music, no inner dialogue—and invite your intuition to give you a sign of how it will guide you.
- Listen.

We Are All Connected Bath

ALL DIRECTIONS, ALL ELEMENTS, ALL SEASONS, ALL SIGNS
TEA PAIRING: BASIL AND ROSE TEA

Maybe we are all here at this time to grow and to help each other grow. The light we see in others is really just a reflection of our own. The darkness shadow we see in others is really just a reflection of our own. Maybe everything we think, say, and act on creates a ripple effect. Maybe our unique spirit is a drop in an ocean of collective consciousness. Maybe we are all here at this time to work through something massive and collective together. Maybe that is what our ancestors were doing as well. Maybe we come back again and again because we have more to learn.

When I see someone come in for their first Medicine Reading with a bit of indigo in their aura, I know they can feel this great connection. I know they are a teacher for our collective consciousness. If you have ever met someone and felt like you already know them, if you have ever been somewhere that feels eerily familiar, or get really strong déjà vu, I think this is the influence of indigo in your aura. This is the deep connection you feel to unity consciousness speaking up, an energy that is often called psychic. Maybe you are able to see through time and space, maybe you are able to see through another's eyes and hear the whispers of truth the ancestors have for us. Maybe it feels almost effortless to you to interpret your dreams, to receive guidance on what is to come.

If this energy comes naturally to you, use it for good! You have come here to teach, to guide, to focus on the medicine that your deep wisdom and understanding has to teach in unity consciousness. This bath can help you to tap into the feeling of being one with everything.

Ingredients

1 cup Epsom salt

A tub tea of mugwort

10 drops of jasmine, 5 drops of sweet orange, and 5 drops of sandalwood essential oils

1 Adirondack Blue potato, sliced

Labradorite crystal

Ritual

- Place all the ingredients in the bath at a temperature of your choosing.
- Create a smudge using white sage by putting it in a nonflammable tray of some kind and igniting it. Waft the smoke around your body using a feather you have found.
- Step into the bath and dunk your head underwater.
- Place the labradorite crystal on your forehead.
- Think back to your earliest memory. Try to remember before that and before that.
- Notice if there is a common thread or a similar message in each version of the memory you have as you open up space for yourself to remember. What are you meant to hear? What are you mean to teach?
- Sit and soak in the magic and medicine of unity consciousness.

Sacred Rebel Bath

WEST, WATER, AUTUMN, SCORPIO
TEA PAIRING: LEMONGRASS, ROSE, AND NETTLE TEA

No matter where you come from, our human conditioning is geared toward suspicion rather than trust when it comes to other people. I think of my daughter, who can just go up and talk to anyone, so unafraid and so trusting. I wish she could keep that confidence, but it is something that most of us lose by the time we are three.

One of the reasons indigo aura people have such an uncanny ability to accept, look at, and learn from the shadow is because they have experienced a lot of it. Most people with an indigo aura have experienced an incredibly tumultuous time in their youth. Because of this they have a very difficult time trusting people. It can even take them years in an intimate relationship before they trust their partners. I don't think it's healthy to go through life so guarded. I think the key is to see the shadow in people but to remain open anyway. Trust before suspecting. This is wise innocence at its greatest. Stay open to new people and experiences. We might get hurt, yes, but who knows, we might also be pleasantly surprised. This is a bath to remember your wise innocence.

Ingredients

1 cup pink Himalayan sea salt

A tub tea of lemongrass

Pink rose petals

20 drops each of lemon balm and
    rose essential oils

Rose quartz crystal

Ritual

- Place all the ingredients in the bath at a temperature of your choosing.
- Light a candle.
- Create a smudge using palo santo by putting it in a nonflammable tray of some kind and igniting it. Waft the smoke around your body using a feather you have found.
- Step into the bath and dunk your head underwater.
- Place the rose quartz crystal on your belly.

- Trust the water to support you, the herbs to heal you, the salt to cleanse you, and the crystal to hold you.
- Soak in the energy you've created.

7

Violet

When people have the understanding that their internal reality creates their external reality, that they are a drop in one large ocean of consciousness, they usually have the color violet around them. I see violet in places that have a powerful spiritual energy and in the aura of most young children, those who aren't afraid to stay true to who they are.

When I walk through certain places—ancient forests, deserts, and mountains or ruins where people have done a lot of praying—everything becomes a vivid violet hue. To me violet is a color we could all call into our auras to help us feel more connected to all that is.

THE LIGHT

Violets are dreamers and full of good ideas. They are in commune with spirit and no matter what religion they were raised in, they have their own form of connecting to their spirituality. If you are a Violet, you take time to make decisions, and overall you take your time in life. You are drastically affected by the lunar cycles and planetary influences. You create from the channeled messages you receive from the divine. I love seeing a combination of violet and other colors in an aura. For example, red and violet usually surround high-powered innovators, amazing business minds, and great artists and writers.

THE SHADOW

The shadow side of violet is that you may have a hard time grounding dreams into reality. Often brilliant ideas that have been circling around you for months, even years, can get stuck in the etheric realm. You have a tendency toward too many out-of-body experiences, such as smoking weed or experimenting with many psychedelics, without actually processing the messages and medicine from these experiences. Because of the deep spiritual influences of the color violet in the aura, a lavender hue in the aura can indicate grief. Not the acute grief of someone very close to you passing away, but grief as a consistent emotion. The thing you are grieving changes form, but the grief never really disappears.

VIOLET BATHS

DREAM MEDICINE BATH

NEW MOON BATH

GRIEF BATH

FULL MOON BATH

UNITY BATH

DIVINE GUIDANCE BATH

SPIRIT CLEANSING BATH

MERCURY DIRECT BATH

Dream Medicine Bath

WATER, WEST, WINTER, CANCER
TEA PAIRING: LINDEN, VIOLET, AND ROSE TEA

We receive so many powerful messages in our dream state, whether lying down at night or drifting off into a daydream. If you haven't been dreaming lately, check to see that you aren't engaging in practices that steal your dreams. Smoking of any kind replaces the communication your own spirit has with the spirit of what you are smoking. Watching too much TV, spending too much time online, and repressing feelings can also block your dreams from being clear to you. This bath is designed to help you retain and receive the guidance and medicine within and all around us as we dream. Take this bath just before bedtime.

Ingredients

3 cups Epsom salt

A tub tea of mugwort, linden, violet, and calea zacatechichi

Pink and white rose petals

5 drops of violet, 5 drops of lilac, and 10 drops of rose essential oils

Amethyst and lemurian seed crystal

Ritual

- Place all the ingredients in the bath at a temperature of your choosing.
- Create a smudge using cinnamon and palo santo by putting them in a nonflammable tray of some kind and igniting them. Waft the smoke around your body using a feather you have found.
- Step into the bath and dunk your head underwater.
- Place the lemurian seed quartz in your right hand, the amethyst on your heart, and a piece of wet fresh mugwort from the tub tea on the space between your eyebrows.
- Take seven deep *ujjayi* breaths.
- Sit and soak in the dream you've created for yourself.

New Moon Bath

EAST, WIND, SPRING, AQUARIUS, LIBRA, PISCES
TEA PAIRING: CALENDULA, OAT STRAW, RED RASPBERRY LEAF,
AND LEMON BALM TEA

Sometimes on the new moon, the seeds we've planted burst open and inspiration for how to nurture our intentions and grow springs forth. There is a feeling of being so full that we can't stay small any longer.

I've been writing this book for about ten years and ten days. I had the idea to write a book about aura colors ten years ago. I started taking notes and writing down insights. I was in a very violet and dreamy place with it, letting it all come in slowly. I knew the baths were going to be a huge part of it, because I see baths as one of the most accessible ways of being your own healer. Then a while later, two book agents that I really connected with reached out to me. They asked me to put together a book proposal for my Ritual Baths. I put the proposal together in about a month, but then was too nervous to hand it in for another year. When I finally built up the courage to hand it in, they loved it and so did my editor. I was so pumped from the positive momentum that was building up around the proposal that I thought I would be able to get started on it right away.

But when I sat down to write, something felt very wrong. I couldn't stop fidgeting and distracting myself. I felt really off. On the February new moon, I set an intention of courage. I woke up the next day, realizing that the reason I couldn't write the book was because the organization in the proposal didn't feel right for me. The book had to be organized by aura color, the intuitive access point closest to me, and what I'd been working on all along. I had to scrap almost everything I had already written and start fresh. This entire book was written in ten days; each day, I woke up easily before the sun, at a time when my spirit could speak to me the loudest. The words and the messages just poured out of me. I didn't feel afraid. I felt extremely inspired and so full that I couldn't stay small any longer.

This bath is designed to help you to connect to that feeling of expansion, to cultivate the understanding that you have all the guidance you need within you. Let yourself grow as you are meant to.

Ingredients

1 cup Epsom salt

A tub tea of calendula, oat straw, red raspberry leaf, and lemon balm

1 cup red clay

Red rose petals

Copper ball

5 drops of sweet orange and 10 drops of lavender essential oils

River obsidian crystal

Lemurian seed crystal

Rainbow moonstone crystal

Ritual

- Place all the ingredients in the bath at a temperature of your choosing.
- Create a smudge using palo santo by putting it in a nonflammable tray of some kind and igniting it. Waft the smoke around your body using a feather you have found.
- Step into the bath and dunk your head underwater.
- Place the crystals on your body and in your hands.
- Close your eyes and walk yourself through a guided meditation of your own creation.
- Know that the possibilities are endless.
- Soak in the medicine of what inspires you.

Grief Bath

WATER, WEST, AUTUMN, CANCER, PISCES, VIRGO
TEA PAIRING: SELF-HEAL, VIOLET LEAF, LINDEN BLOSSOM, AND NETTLE TEA

I don't know if grief ever truly goes away. I think it's something that we experience and then spend the rest of our lives and beyond processing. No grief is insignificant. If you're feeling it, then it is valid. Even if you are grieving a lost material object, it is valid. I see a milky light purple color around people who are grieving. Sometimes they are grieving the loss of a loved one or the loss of a relationship, job, or home. Taking time to acknowledge grief is powerful medicine.

The last time I saw my sweet cousin whom I lived with when I was kid, I saw this lavender color around him. He had suffered a long-endured childhood trauma and continued to be tormented by it throughout his life. He turned to heroin to escape the darkness and pain. I invited him to come stay with us, and I offered to bring him down to the Amazon, where plant medicine is used to cure addiction. But he assured me he was doing better. I wanted to believe him, and I also wanted to respect his boundaries. On the way to his funeral, I knew better, but also couldn't help but blame myself for not being more persistent in helping him. It was an opportunity to practice what I preach and to understand that this guilt mixed with grief is a shadow energy. This shadow is a powerful way to gain wisdom. The bath that I'm sharing here is the one I made for his mother, my aunt, when I went to see her right after I found out about his death.

I understand that throughout my life I've needed to see and experience so much shadow in order to choose to stay really close to the light. Maybe, by doing so, I can set an example for others to do the same. I couldn't help my beloved cousin, but I can hope that maybe there are other silent sufferers out there who see my work and it helps them through their day. I think it's important to share some of the painful aspects of life, because they are part of what helps us appreciate the beauty. It also lets us know this: "You are not alone. Even if I never met you, I am here for you."

I think it's sad that our culture has no room for grief. In my world I would let everyone have at least three months, or better yet, a year off of work after we've lost someone very close to us. Because we don't have that, I think it's important to find ways to show up for people we know are grieving. Cry with them, hold space for them, be there. I know that it feels uncomfortable, that we feel like we don't know what to say or do. Even if people who are grieving yell at you, they will always remember who was by their side during that painful time in their lives. I'm learning in this lifetime how to show up more. Maybe there is someone you can show up for today too. Maybe it's you.

Grief comes in waves. Some days we are doing fine and some days it hits us hard and brings us to our knees. This bath is designed to help us process and integrate our grief or hurt just a little bit less. If you know someone who is grieving, maybe you can make this bath for them.

Ingredients

1 cup Epsom salt

A tub tea of self-heal, violet leaf, linden blossom, and nettles

5 drops each of violet and jasmine essential oils mixed into 1 cup each of milk and honey (any kind)

Purple and yellow rose petals

Rose and smoky quartz crystals

Ritual

- Place all the ingredients in the bath at a temperature of your choosing.
- Light a candle and as you do, send a blessing to anyone you've loved and lost.
- Create a smudge using palo santo by putting it in a nonflammable tray of some kind and igniting it. Waft the smoke around your body using a feather you have found.
- Step into the bath and dunk your head underwater.
- Take several deep, cleansing breaths.
- Invite cleansing tears to come.
- Soak in the medicine you have created.

Full Moon Bath

ALL ELEMENTS, ALL DIRECTIONS, ALL SEASONS, ALL SIGNS
TEA PAIRING: NETTLE, ANGELICA, AND ROSE TEA

When the veils are thinning and the full moon is rising, we are being called more and more to walk in the light and awareness of love. During this time, we are tapping into our instinctual nature and really taking in the omens we receive on our path. The full moon is sending us many lessons. If we are trusting the universe, they can be soft and gentle. The longer we stay in our minds, future focused or past obsessed, the louder and stronger the omens must be. The universe wants us to be safe, protected, and nurtured, and that is why we get so many signs. This bath is designed to help you get quiet enough to process the omens you're receiving. You know what you need to do; now all you have to find is the courage to do it.

Ingredients

3 cups Epsom salt

A tub tea of nettle and angelica

White sage leaves

1 cup coconut milk

Red and pink rose petals

3 drops of palo santo essential oil

Obsidian crystal

Ritual

- Place all the ingredients in the bath at a temperature of your choosing.
- Light candles in the bathroom.
- Cleanse your aura with a selenite wand.
- Step into the bath and dunk your head underwater.
- Release three deep sighs.
- Close your eyes and breathe in slow, rhythmic breaths for fifteen minutes.
- Soak in the full moon medicine you've created.

Unity Bath

ALL ELEMENTS, ALL DIRECTIONS, ALL SEASONS, ALL SIGNS
TEA PAIRING: ROSE, JASMINE, LINDEN, AND VIOLET TEA

If it is happiness you desire, then let yourself be happy. If it is connectedness you desire, let yourself feel how completely connected you are. Step out of the shadow of yourself. Stop hiding. You are beautiful, be your beautiful self entirely. You are powerful; allow yourself to be empowered!

If you stop holding yourself back, your angels will all notice and stand encircled around you to cheer you on. Let your joyful heart lead your path. Have gratitude for every birth you've experienced and every death that has brought you there.

Dear One, you are not meant to feel repressed. Step out of the dualistic thinking of good and bad. Where there is light, by universal law, there must also be darkness. It is you who must choose your light, your power of joy. No one else can do this for you! You won't need to tell anyone because your eyes, your actions, and your presence will say it all. Don't be afraid, the change will be great. Change brings some pain, but trust it will improve all your relations. Especially your relationship with the world you've created for yourself.

Ingredients

1 cup Epsom salt

1 cup coconut milk

Pink rose petals

10 drops of jasmine essential oil

Rose quartz crystal

Ritual

- Place all the ingredients in the bath at a temperature of your choosing.
- Create a smudge using white sage by putting it in a nonflammable tray of some kind and igniting it. Waft the smoke around your body using a feather you have found.
- Step into the bath.
- Breathe in. You are the universe. Breathe out. You are the universe.
- Breathe in the way your actions affect the universe. Breathe out compassion.
- Sit and soak in the beautiful energy you've created.

Divine Guidance Bath

WIND, EAST, AUTUMN, ALL SIGNS
TEA PAIRING: RED CLOVER, DANDELION,
AND NETTLE TEA OR A GLASS OF RED WINE

Once, a long time ago, there was a wise Zen master. People from far and near would seek his counsel and ask for his wisdom. One day an important man, a man used to commanding and obedience, came to visit the master. "I have come today to ask you to teach me about Zen. Open my mind to enlightenment." The Zen master smiled and said that they should discuss the matter over a cup of tea. He poured and he poured and the tea rose to the rim and began to spill over the table and finally onto the robes of the wealthy man. Finally the visitor shouted, "Enough. You are spilling the tea all over. Can't you see the cup is full?" The master stopped pouring and smiled at his guest and said, "You are like this tea cup, so full that nothing more can be added. Come back to me when the cup is empty."
—ANCIENT ZEN STORY

But how do we empty the cup? When our spiritual cup is too full, we can feel exhaustion and stress. If we cannot empty it, it flows over into the emotions, and when our emotional cup is too full, we can feel anxiety or depression. If we can't empty it emotionally, then it flows into the mind; when our mental cup is too full we can feel our busy mind take over. If we can't empty the cup mentally, it flows into the body, and when our physical cup is cluttered, we experience illness. This is our brilliant body's way of cleansing energy for us and getting us to pay attention.

This bath is designed to help you to take a moment to empty your cup so that you can prepare and create space for the intentions you will set moving forward.

Ingredients

1 cup Epsom salt

Peonies

1 cup red wine (you can substitute apple cider vinegar)

10 drops of lavender and 5 drops of sandalwood essential oils

Labradorite crystal

Clear quartz crystal

Ruby crystal

Ritual

- Place all the ingredients in the bath at a temperature of your choosing.
- Cleanse your aura with a selenite wand.
- Step into the bath.
- Touch the surface of the water and say, "I can create space because I'm created of space."
- Soak in the powerful energy you've created.

Spirit Cleansing Bath

EAST, WIND, SPRING, LIBRA
TEA PAIRING: VIOLET AND HIBISCUS TEA

Sometimes we don't quite have the energetic boundaries in place to realize what is or is not our energy. We end up carrying with us the energy of others, making it our own and letting it drain us. Sensitive people can easily read the people around them. Instead of embodying ourselves, we have the ability to show up as who others need us to be and say what others need us to say. We can even lower our vibration, engaging in self-destructive activities with others just so that person doesn't feel alone. These practices drain us.

We do this because the healer within, the compassionate one, has just witnessed pain and suffering and thinks that it is our responsibility to fix or carry it. But carrying others' energy can result in weight gain, skin irritations, lack of sleep, unexplained mood swings, and autoimmune deficiencies. To me there is no difference between what is happening spiritually, emotionally, mentally, or physically. Most imbalances usually begin from a spiritual place, then seep into the emotions, then into the mind, and finally into our physical bodies. Just like we have a physical immune system, we also have a spiritual immune system. If our physical immune system is weakened, we are guided to take a look at whether we are engaging in relationships or activities that are energetically draining us. By the time something has become physical it has probably been brewing in the spirit for a while.

Even when we practice being constantly aware and ever present, we can have moments in which we are caught off guard, find ourselves bumping into unwanted energy, and maybe even taking it on. When we cleanse our minds, we naturally cleanse our bodies. When we cleanse our bodies, we naturally cleanse our minds. When we cleanse our spirits, we become open to receiving the messages about how to cleanse the mind and body.

When I was in my shamanic training in the Amazon, my teacher would often send me dark energy during ceremonies so I could learn how to defend myself from it. Despite all the different talismans and instruments I would use, I could not prevent the dark visions and fear. I could not figure out why protecting myself was so hard. After a year of these dark visions, I finally realized that the darkness wasn't coming from outside of me; what I was seeing was the disregarded fear and shadow energy within me. The next ceremony, when the dark visions and feelings of fear came through, I asked myself, What is the one thing I already have within me? What is the one gift, the one talisman, that moves with me wherever I go? What is more powerful than fear?

And I realized that the answer was LOVE.

I focused really strongly on my two dogs, because at that time, they were what I loved most in this world. To me they were the archetypes of love that I could envision. And you know what happened? The dark visions disappeared and were replaced with light and beauty.

To me, love is the most powerful force, the most powerful energy there is. No matter what challenges you are facing, if you focus on love, then you will find healing and balance on the other end of those challenges. Remember to embody yourself, know yourself, love and accept yourself. Check to see if you're nervous about being judged. What others think of you is not your business. Stop worrying about what others are thinking, feeling, or doing. Be who you need you to be and not who others need you to be. This will give you confidence and help you keep your energy and not take on others' energy as if it were your own. You can cleanse your spirit. You can be your own healer. This bath can help.

Ingredients

3 cups black lava salt

A tub tea of violet leaf and flower, white sage, mugwort, lavender, and hibiscus

Amethyst crystal powder

10 drops each of lavender and sweet orange essential oils

Purple rose petals

Fresh violet leaves and flowers

Ritual

- Place all the ingredients in the bath at a temperature of your choosing.
- Light a candle.
- Create a smudge using white sage by putting it in a nonflammable tray of some kind and igniting it. Waft the smoke around your body using a feather you have found.
- Step into the bath and dunk your head underwater.
- Focus on what you love most and keep your focus.
- Don't let yourself get distracted.
- Feel this love travel within and around you.
- Soak in the cleansing protection of love.

Mercury Direct Bath

NORTH, EARTH, WINTER, SAGITTARIUS
TEA PAIRING: ELDERBERRY, ROSE HIP, AND LICORICE TEA

Mercury Retrograde can have an intense effect on the color of violet within you. When Mercury finally turns direct again, meet this transition with feeling grateful for the rest and a very deep lesson learned. Mercury Retrograde can bring up a lot for us. This bath is designed to help you cleanse, process, and digest the revelations, emotions, and sluggishness this period can bestow upon us and get you ready for positive forward momentum. This is a bath for tapping back into the flow.

Ingredients

1 cup Epsom salt

1 cup charcoal

Petals from 2 daffodil flowers

1 cup pink rose petals

1 tablespoon maqui berry powder

10 drops each of rose and rosemary essential oils

Smoky quartz and obsidian crystal

Ritual

- Place all the ingredients in the bath at a temperature of your choosing.
- Create a smudge using white sage by putting it in a nonflammable tray of some kind and igniting it. Waft the smoke around your body using a feather you have found.
- Step into the bath and dunk your head underwater.
- Take three cleansing breaths, exhaling with a sigh.
- Say into the water, "I surrender," three times.
- Sit and soak in the powerful energy you've created.

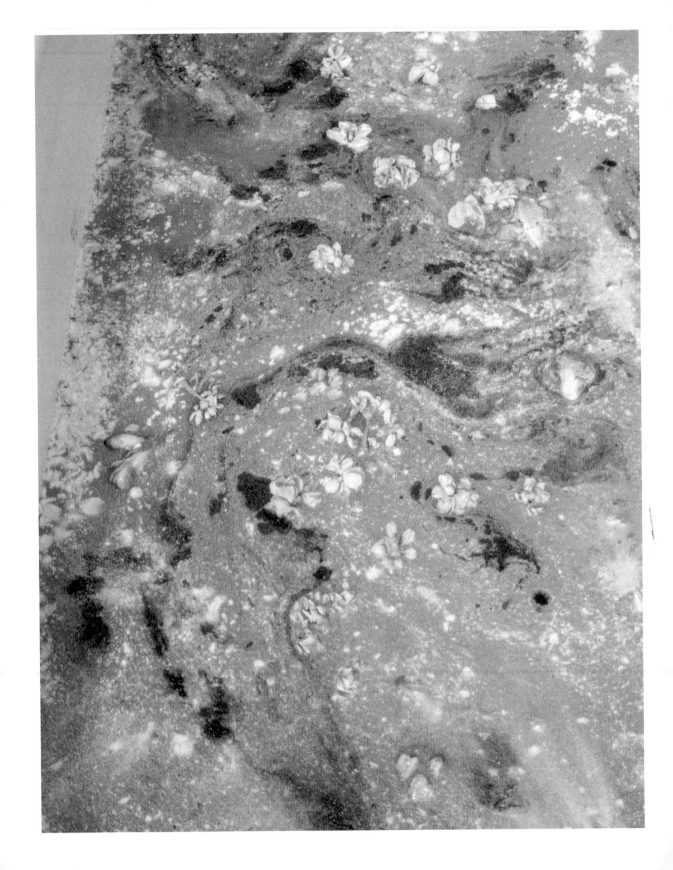

8

The Accent Colors

The accent colors are colors that appear as more of a hue
in a person's aura along with other stronger aura colors.
The accent colors are also more rare.

SILVER
De-Armor Yourself Bath

GOLD
Mandala Ritual Bath

OPALESCENT
Past Lives Bath

MAGENTA
New Love Bath

Silver

Silver is a rare color to see in the aura, and it usually means strong protection, like armor. This is the kind of protection that comes in for someone who has perhaps felt a bit alone or unloved in life. Sometimes Silvers are not meant to feel supported by other people because they have the love and support that comes from their guides and guardians. They have strength gained from presence, persistence, and patience. They have a medicine of resilience to share with the world. Often Silvers are the ones sharing their stories of survival, not from a place of victim consciousness, but from a place of endurance and stamina.

THE LIGHT

I like seeing this color around people who have just experienced some kind of trauma or are finally ready to heal the trauma of their past. They are armoring themselves up so they are not hurt again.

THE SHADOW

To go through life always armored means you are not letting anything in or out. Always prepared for war, a silver aura will attack first and think later.

De-Armor Yourself Bath

NORTH, EARTH, WINTER, AIRES
TEA PAIRING: ROSE, NETTLE, HAWTHORN BERRY, AND CINNAMON TEA

What if instead of carrying this heavy armor around with you all the time you replaced it with an armor of light? So all that comes to and from you is light? You no longer have to be so wounded, because the light will heal you if you let it. With this new armor of light, you can let the light of love heal you like it wants to.

Ingredients

1 cup Epsom salt

2 tablespoons charcoal powder

1 teaspoon mica powder

White rose petals

1 tablespoon colloidal silver

A few drops each of eucalyptus and lavender essential oils

The Dream: Lightning struck quartz

The Dream: Blue pansy flowers

Ritual

- Place all the ingredients in the bath at a temperature of your choosing.
- Light a candle.
- Create a smudge using palo santo by putting it in a nonflammable tray of some kind and igniting it. Waft the smoke around your body using a feather you have found.
- Step into the bath and dunk your head underwater.
- Close your eyes and call in your guides and guardians.
- If you have just experienced some trauma and are feeling a bit raw, ask your guides to give you some gentle armor of silver light to protect you while you heal.
- If you feel you've been overly protective of yourself to the point of being defensive, ask them to help you remove your armor and replace it with light.
- See yourself in your mind's eye surrounded by a soft silver light.
- Sit and soak in the feeling of being held and protected.

Gold

Gold in the aura is the highest form of protection. This is someone who can see bad things happening all around but remains protected from them. This is someone who is well loved not only by people in the third dimension, but also by their guides and guardians. Gold in the aura signifies health, abundance, and confidence.

THE LIGHT

Plain and simple, gold is protection.

THE SHADOW

Golds sometimes don't always realize or feel worthy of how easy life is meant to be for them.

Mandala Ritual Bath

WATER, WEST, SUMMER, LEO
TEA PAIRING: PALO SANTO, CINNAMON, AND ROSE TEA

Like the sun and the moon, I'm just a reflection of you. Whatever you see in me is within you.

Nature offers us so much balance if we let her. For example, getting lost as you look into the face of a sunflower and in that same moment tuning in to how connected we all are. Dear One, you are the sunflower. Be the beauty that you are! Don't forget the truth of who you are. You are love. The light you see is there to encourage you, the shadow you see is there to give you wisdom. This is unity consciousness. If we are disconnected individually, then our human family will be too. Take some time to yourself and ground down into the strength of your softness. Find the mandalas that nature offers us, like our sister the moon and the constellations that surround her. Weave their story into the essence of your being. This bath can assist you in letting unity grow. When you are finished, go outside and smile at a stranger.

Ingredients

1 cup Epsom salt
1 cup red alaea salt
A tub tea of palo santo, saffron, and calendula
Sunflowers

1 cup coconut milk with 5 drops each of frankincense, palo santo, and rose absolute essential oils
1 tablespoon gold mica powder
Rose quartz crystal

Ritual

- Place all the ingredients in the bath at a temperature of your choosing.
- Light a candle.
- Create a smudge using copal by putting it in a nonflammable tray of some kind and igniting it. Waft the smoke around your body using a feather you have found.
- Step into the bath and dunk your head underwater.

- Let yourself take deep breaths until you feel ready to relax into meditation.
- As you are dropping into meditation, go through the people, animals, plants, stones, and places on Earth that you know love you and that you love.
- Pick up a sunflower and take at least five minutes to stare into it, letting it become you.
- Feel yourself surrounded by the protection that this love gives you.

Opalescent

This is a color I often see around well-known people or people who are meant to be in the spotlight because they have so much inner beauty it's meant to pour outward. They have a very angelic energy, and could have spent time in a past life in a different dimension. Angelic energy is an energy that has come to help us, that is here to look out for others. People can have angels appear in their auras who may be ancestors that are now our angels, children who have left this Earth too early or have been lost through miscarriage, animals who have passed, and also angelic multidimensional beings who love and look out for us.

That being said, sometimes angels need to ground down into human form and do their work in the third dimension. These people have a base opalescent look in their auras. Animals almost always have opal auras and that's why I think animals are angels. I put opalescent in the accent colors because it's very, very rare to see. I also often see someone's aura turn opalescent before they are about to perform a selfless or heroic act or really show up for another person.

This is the kind of person who can pick up just about anything and be very good at it. People are naturally attracted to them and even if they are working a humble job, they have an air of royalty to them.

Call this color into your aura when you are ready to let the light of love shine through you. Opalescents have been through a lot in this life and in past lives. They choose to let their light shine because they have experienced the consequences of what happens when they don't. They are slow to cut people out of their lives, no matter how much harm that person may intend for them, because they know how much it hurts to lose people. Because they magnetize everything and everyone, they will have lights shutting down around them, things falling off shelves, and even birds flying toward their heads.

THE LIGHT

Opalescents have a call to use their magnetism for good. They are the celebrities and artists you see using their gifts to wield positive change in the world. They know they are role models and they take that responsibility seriously, always considering the example they are setting.

THE SHADOW

Because of the sheer magnetism of these people, they can often attract jealousy. People assume everything has been easy for them, when usually that is anything but the truth. Since they are always being watched and looked up to, any little thing they do that is questionable creates an enormous ripple effect. Opalescents can often feel very lonely, like no one understands them, and sometimes the people closest to them are the people most jealous of them.

Past Lives Bath

NORTH, EARTH, WINTER, SCORPIO, CANCER
TEA PAIRING: WHITE PINE AND ROSE TEA

The truth is no one can say for sure what happens when we die. That's why death and where we were before we were born is called the great mystery. That being said, I have a feeling that when we die, if we understand that we have died, our spirit returns to the great mystery to clear itself, integrate, and process the lessons learned in life. If we have more to learn, we come back. If we have a message to share with the world, we come back.

If you talk to very young children, they sometimes can remember their past lives and they can tell you all about who they used to be, even what their name was. Lifetime to lifetime we often return to the same soul cluster, the people we knew in previous lifetimes, because we have some work to do with them, both personally and for the collective consciousness.

There are some people we meet who make us feel afraid or very angry immediately. It could be because they have harmed us in a previous life. Or sometimes we meet people and feel totally enamored by them; we love them. Maybe we have loved before. Even our beloved animals can return to us in other forms; I think the animals that come to us are our angels, who need to land in the third dimension to heal, protect, and soothe our spirits.

I wonder if the people and animals we meet, homes we live in, places we travel to, and items we collect are not somehow guided by our past life experiences. Even if they are not conscious of it, Opalescents are very connected to their past lives and they have usually had very powerful ones. Lifetime after lifetime they come back to set an example of divine love for people. They are very good at trusting their intuition, knowing which projects to take and knowing who to talk to.

Call opal into your aura when you are ready to take the wisdom that you've integrated into your wise spirit from many lifetimes and share it with the world. This bath is designed to help you tap into your angelic energy.

Ingredients

1 cup Epsom salt

A tub tea of linden, violet, and white pine

Fresh white pine needles

White and purple rose petals

Frankincense and jasmine essential oils mixed into 4 liters milk and 3 tablespoons honey

Common opal

Ritual

- Place all the ingredients in the bath at a temperature of your choosing.
- Light a candle.
- Create a smudge using white sage by putting it in a nonflammable tray of some kind and igniting it. Waft the smoke around your body using a feather you have found.
- Cleanse your aura with a selenite wand.
- Step into the bath and dunk your head underwater.
- Hold the opal in your left hand.
- Ask the wisdom of the water, the plants, the stones, and your own beautiful spirit to show you anything you may need to work with, heal, and integrate from a past life.
- Sit, soak, and receive the teachings.

Magenta

Magenta is the color of newfound love. While this usually indicates newfound romantic love, it can also be a newfound love of life or indicate pregnancy, because carrying a baby in your womb is an embrace of new love. This is the one color that brings with it such a positive energy, I don't really see light and shadow in it; all I can see is the excitement of new love. This doesn't necessarily mean a new romantic partner; when you are in a healthy long-term relationship, you get waves of newfound love for your partner over the course of time. Magenta also means that this newfound love is giving you a lot of energy to complete the projects that are in your highest good. Make the necessary moves you need to make in life to celebrate this new love completely.

THE LIGHT

Magentas set the example of new love, butterflies in the tummy, synchronicities, the dawn of hope, and new beginnings.

THE SHADOW

Magentas that haven't harnessed their energy can get caught up in pipe dreams, projections, and unrequited love.

New Love Bath

EAST, WIND, SPRING, GEMINI
TEA PAIRING: ROSE, ROSE HIP, LINDEN, VIOLET LEAF AND FLOWER TEA

This bath is designed for calling new love into your life. Maybe you are at a point in your relationship where you feel you've hit a wall and the growth together has stagnated. Maybe you are ready to take the next step with that special someone you have a really good feeling about. Maybe you want to connect to the baby growing in your belly. Open up and let the fresh wave of energy come in with all the new love it carries.

Ingredients

1 cup Epsom salt

1 cup dragon fruit powder

1 cup coconut milk

10 drops of rose absolute essential oil

Rose quartz crystal

Ritual

- Place all the ingredients in the bath at a temperature of your choosing.
- Light a candle.
- Create a smudge using palo santo and cinnamon by putting them in a nonflammable tray of some kind and igniting them. Waft the smoke around your body using a feather you have found.
- Step into the bath and dunk your head underwater.
- Place the rose quartz crystal on that big beautiful heart of yours.
- Sit and soak in the magic and medicine you've created.

In Closing

Thank you for participating in being your own healer with the power of Ritual Baths. I began posting my baths on social media in 2013, and I'm happy that so many people have been inspired by my work and are sharing their baths with the world as well. I work hard to set an example of being my own healer, and I love to see it taking root and growing. I hope you feel inspired to share your baths or any insight you have gained from this book with the world. You can do this through photos you take or by preparing a bath that you found to be powerful for someone you love.

I think there are only a few ingredients you need to truly be your own healer: kindness, compassion, and dedication. The access point to our inner healer is kindness. The marking of a true healer is one who puts kindness above being right, above being admired, above everything.

It's not about where you come from, how many distant lands you've traveled to in your pursuit of healing, how many certifications you have, your accent, your outfit, your occupation, or whether you are aware that we are all each other's as well as our own healers. If you are practicing kindness to yourself and others, you are practicing healing. If you are dedicated to growing more and more compassionate toward yourself and others, you are practicing healing.

I'm truly grateful to all of my Medicine Reading clients who have taught me so much. I'm looking forward to growing on this journey.

Gratitude to Mother Earth and Love for being the true masters, the true healers and teachers.

Encyclopedia of Ingredients

Some of these ingredients may be harder to find than others, and like all of the herbs and crystals in this book, it's okay to work with what you have. The most important ingredient in any ritual is your intention. If you don't have all the tools, no worries! All you need is your love. Before any Ritual Bath, it is very powerful to prepare your aura by setting your energy and intention in a way that allows you to be truly ready and open to receiving the medicine of your Ritual Bath.

Either collect fresh herbs and wrap them into a bundle with string and hang them to dry or buy dried herbs. Use them by burning them in a special shell, bowl, or dish; some can also make lovely teas.

Physical healing properties are listed in italics.

FLOWERS, FRUITS, AND VEGETABLES

The Reality

RED ROSE—divine masculine, grounding, supportive, vitamin C, *immunity-boosting, diuretic*

....

WHITE ROSE—wise innocence, new beginnings

....

PINK ROSE—divine feminine, creative, inspiring

....

YELLOW ROSE—kindness

....

WHITE PINE NEEDLES—opens connection to all dimensions, support, *lung, cough, and cold healer*

....

RED POTATO—soothing, grounding, nourishing, *potassium, vitamin C, vitamin B$_6$, ulcer healer*

....

PURPLE POTATO—heals disconnection with ancestors, *potassium, vitamin C, vitamin B$_6$, ulcer healer*

....

RED APPLES—abundance, patience, magnesium, vitamin C, vitamin B$_6$, and fiber

....

BLOOD ORANGE—inspiring, surprising, uplifting, *vitamin C*

....

RASPBERRIES—life energy, sweetness, joy

....

ROSEMARY—soft, motherly, energetic protection

....

FRESH BASIL—activating, stimulating, abundance

....

ORANGES—enlivening, grounding in joy, inspiring

....

PEACHES—sexual healing, nourishment, comfort

....

CUCUMBERS—cooling, refreshing

....

LEMON—powerful energy cleanser

....

MIXED BERRIES—enlivening

....

DANDELION GREENS—supportively clears anger and frustration

....

BLACKBERRIES—motivating

....

BLUEBERRIES—meditation, communication, mediumship

....

THYME—clears stagnation from grief

....

ORANGE PEELS—motivating

....

OAK LEAVES—wisdomkeepers, guidance, possibilities

....

ROWAN LEAVES—protection from other dimensions, power

....

VANILLA EXTRACT—soothing, kindness, sweetness

....

EUCALYPTUS LEAVES—activating, awakening, cleansing, refreshing

....

The Dream

VANILLA BEAN ORCHID—love, enchantment

....

GRAPE LEAVES—abundance, children

....

RED CLOVERS—fertility

....

BLACK-EYED SUSAN—fertility, growth, confidence

ECHINACEA—healing, dreams, vision, spiritual immunity

EVENING PRIMROSE—healing, heals wounds

SNAPDRAGON—joy

CHERRY BLOSSOM—fresh energy

WATERMELON—abundance, celebration

FORSYTHIA—promise, hope

DAISIES—joy, light, prosperity

SUNFLOWERS—meditation, encouragement, a mirror

YARROW FLOWERS—healing pain, grief, and fear

FORGET-ME-NOTS—patience, love

DAFFODILS—endurance, stamina, courage

PEONIES—attract kindness, beauty, and truth

BLUE PANSIES—dream space

....

FRESH VIOLET LEAVES—divine love

....

BLUE HYDRANGEA—connection to community

....

CORNFLOWERS—prolific growth

....

PURPLE ROSE—dreams

....

TUB TEA HERBS

The Reality

GREEN TEA—cleansing

....

ROSEMARY—protecting

....

KAVA—relaxing

....

MUGWORT—wisdom, dreams

....

WHITE PINE—strengthening

....

CARDAMOM PODS—warmth, ease with change

CINNAMON STICKS—protection

CHAI TEA—inspiring, growth, productivity

PASSION FRUIT—new love in your life

GOLDENROD—immunity

CHAMOMILE—calming

The Dream

ELDERBERRIES—community, friendship

SHATAVARI—divine feminine

THYME—processing grief

HIBISCUS—stimulates gratitude

ROSE HIP—immunity, fertility, change

RED RASPBERRY LEAF—maternal healer

NETTLES—doubt clearer

SAFFRON—loyalty

LEMON BALM—calming

LINDEN—sweetness of love

VIOLET—dreams, love manifestation

ST. JOHN'S WORT—uplifting

WAYUSA—uplifting

RED CLOVER—fertility, growth

EVENING PRIMROSE—wound healer

ECHINACEA—energetic immunity

BLACK-EYED SUSAN—energy clearer

OSHA ROOT—addiction cleansing

CHRYSANTHEMUM—grounding

VALERIAN—heals pain

YARROW—pain release, growth

CHAMOMILE—calming

WILD ROSE—wild abundant love

SELF-HEAL—be your own healer

CAT'S CLAW—protection

ANGELICA—calling in angels

HAWTHORN—aid in heart offerings

MULLEIN—deep breath

ELDERBERRY—healing wisdom

SLIPPERY ELM—spirit soothing

BUTTERFLY PEA FLOWER—magic

CALEA ZACATECHICHI—inspire powerful dreams

OAT STRAW—a blanket of soothing love

ESSENTIAL OILS

The Reality

LAVENDER—for when you want to let go

....

ROSE ABSOLUTE—for the power of your love

....

LEMON BALM—for when you want to keep it calm

....

ROSEMARY—for when you want divine mother protection

....

The Dream

VETIVER—for when you want to get grounded

....

ROSEWOOD—for when you want to feel safe being loved

....

CEDARWOOD—for when you want to feel at home anywhere

....

CARDAMOM—for when you are ready to wake up

....

SWEET ORANGE—for when you want to create from a place of joy

....

VANILLA—for when you want to attract sweetness

....

JASMINE—for when you want to dance with the divine feminine

....

PATCHOULI—for when you want to wake up your sexual self

....

LINDEN BLOSSOM—for when you want to call all things love into your life

....

LEMONGRASS—for when you want to find your voice

....

FRANGIPANI—for when you feel like exploring just how happy you can let yourself be

....

FRANKINCENSE—for when you need a blessing

....

PALO SANTO—for when you need a blessing

....

LEMON BALM—for sweet calm

....

LILAC—for when you feel ready for the new

....

VIOLET—for when you're ready for the love of your life

....

CRYSTALS

The Reality

SMOKY QUARTZ—for when you feel heavy

....

CLEAR QUARTZ—for when you set intentions

....

AMETHYST—for your everything

....

ROSE QUARTZ—for the healing power of love

....

OBSIDIAN—for when you're feeling stuck

....

The Dream

CITRINE—for when you're for abundance

....

CARNELIAN—for when it's time to get to work

....

SAPPHIRE—to speak your truth

....

MOONSTONE—to ground the dreamer

....

LABRADORITE—for when you want healing

....

MOSS AGATE—for when you want to get better with money

....

MALACHITE—for when you want to remember you are love, you are loved

....

EMERALD—for when you want to celebrate

....

JADE—for your truth, guidance, health, and beauty

....

TURQUOISE—for when you want to live your truth

....

TOPAZ—for when you know you need some conscious confrontation

....

BLACK TOURMALINE—for when you need to stop picking up energy that is
no longer yours

....

LARIMAR—for when you want to know your truth

....

BLUE APATITE—for when you need to speak in public

....

CELESTITE—for when you want to interpret your dreams

....

LIGHTNING STRUCK QUARTZ—for when you want to meet your inner shaman

LEMURIAN SEED—for when you want to access the wisdom of your multidimensional spirit

RAINBOW MOONSTONE—for direction on your many dreams

COPPER NUGGET—for when you want to balance out

OPAL—for when you are calling in your angels

EXTRAS, POWDERS/LIQUIDS

HONEY—for when you are ready for all things divine love

APPLE JUICE—for when you want to cleanse

ANY MILKS—for when you want to soothe

CRANBERRY JUICE—for when you want to release old pain

OAT MILK—for when you want to soothe your spirit and your skin

RASPBERRY JUICE—for when you're ready for birthing something or someone

COCONUT MILK—for when you want to soothe

OCEAN WATER—for cleansing wisdom

MOON WATER—for guidance

APPLE CIDER VINEGAR—for when you're ready for balance

ORANGE JUICE—for connecting to your personal power

PEACH JUICE—for finding your sweetness

COPPER POWDER—for when you want to activate something

RED WINE—for when you want to bathe in deep cleansing relaxation

BLUE-GREEN ALGAE—for when you want to feel the abundance of receptivity

BAKING SODA—for when you want to deep-clean your energy

ROSE WATER—for when you want to bathe in the vibration of divine love

DRAGON FRUIT POWDER—for when you are ready to call in new love

GREEN JUICE—for when you need to remember where you come from

RED CLAY—for when your spirit needs nourishment

BENTONITE CLAY—for when you need to be in one place at one time

GRAVIOLA POWDER—for when you are ready to let go of anger

NETTLE LEAF POWDER—for everything, especially protection

PUMPKIN SEED MILK—for when you want to feel like Cinderella, living her best life

STRAWBERRY JUICE—for when you are ready to wake up to the sweetness of life

AÇAÍ AND MAQUI BERRY—for when your spirit wants to dance

MICA POWDER (super sparkle gold, copper, white, majestic gold)—for when you want a very powerful abundant shield

COLLOIDAL SILVER—for when you are ready to find your shield

GOLD MICA—for when you are ready to feel like Yas Queen Yas

CHARCOAL—for when you need to detox

HIBISCUS POWDER—for when you feel on the outside the way you feel within

CRUSHED AMETHYST—for when you want a little extra awareness

CRUSHED LEPIDOLITE—for when you feel like you've been on your phone too much

CRUSHED CELESTITE/LARIMAR/TURQUOISE (blue crystal color)—for when you know it's time to hear your truth

SALTS

EPSOM SALT—For when you want to cleanse your spirit

PINK HIMALAYAN SEA SALT—for when you want to connect to your wisdom

RED ALAEA SALT—for when you want to move your energy

LAVA SALT—for when you feel a little spicy

PERSIAN BLUE SALT—for when you are healing your voice

KITCHEN SALT—for when you want to ground

SMUDGES

The following tools, which are used to cleanse, bless, and protect the aura, each work in a slightly different way, but as long as you are smudging with respect and love you can't go wrong.

Create a tea and transfer it to a spray bottle or burn and use the smoke of the following:

CINNAMON STICKS—for when you need protection, awareness, warmth

PALO SANTO—for when you need blessing, protection, spiritual guidance, peace, calm, and strength

ROSEMARY—for when you want to wake up

LAVENDER—for when you are calling in peace and calm

SELENITE—for when you want to clear your aura of any charged vibes

MUGWORT—for when you want to dream with wolflike protection, inner vision, divine feminine, adaptability, and prolific productivity

PINE—for when you are ready to get well

FRANKINCENSE—for when you want to connect to the divine

SWEETGRASS—for when you want to invite your guides and guardians with warmth, friendliness, gratitude, love, kindness, gentleness, and softening

WHITE SAGE—for when you feel like you want the spiritual equivalent of bleach, protection, prayer, and connection to divine masculinity

ROSE—for when you are calling in love, abundance, prosperity, and protection

CEDAR—for when you're seeking strength, guidance, and grandmother wisdom

WHITE PINE—for when you're seeking guidance

COPAL—for when you want to say thank you

YERBA SANTA—for when you want to cleanse the lungs, process grief, set boundaries, and purify

Crystals are great for when you want a quick, smokeless smudge. I suggest using a wand-shaped crystal that you slowly brush through your auric field in long strokes toward the earth.

Use for Aura Cleansing

SELENITE—for when you want to let go of what is not yours

LEPIDOLITE—for when you've been plugged in for too long

BLACK TOURMALINE—for when you need psychic protection

AMETHYST—for when you are going through a transformation

Use for Aura Blessing

BLUE CALCITE—for when you want to remember your dreams

RAINBOW TOURMALINE—for when you want protection while you shine

AMETHYST—for when you want to celebrate your transformation

THE AURA QUIZ

I am not sure if we can learn to see auras. While I think aura photography is very fun, I don't think it is an accurate depiction of the aura. Things always look different in photographs than they do in person. I believe that when we close our eyes and see color, it is often the color of our own aura that we are seeing. This quiz is a fun way to help you discover the base color of your aura and what baths to take.

WHEN IT COMES TO WORK, I . . .

a. Am driven, focused, and successful.

b. Am more of a creative.

c. Knew what I wanted to be when I was a kid and am doing that work now.

d. Help others and or the planet.

e. Use my gift of discernment and am great at following clues.

f. Teach in some way.

g. Have a hard time figuring out what to do, but I have big ideas for things I'd like to do one day.

h. All of the above.

MY HOME IS . . .

a. In the same area I grew up in, near my family of origin; I've lived in the same place for years.

b. Near the water and a bit messy.

c. My happy place.

d. Wherever the ones I love are.

e. A fun place to have friends over.

f. Quiet and peaceful.

g. Anywhere I go.

h. All of the above.

I FEEL MOST CONNECTED TO MY PURPOSE WHEN . . .

a. I'm planning for the future and future generations.

b. I'm creating.

c. I'm working.

d. I'm caring for others.

e. I'm sharing.

f. I'm at my most intuitive.

g. I'm dreaming.

h. All of the above.

IN LOVE, I'M . . .

a. Very committed.

b. Playful.

c. Loyal.

d. Nurturing.

e. Connected.

f. Impulsive.

g. Connected to the divine.

h. All of the above.

WHEN I'M EXPOSED TO NEW IDEAS AND PLACES, I . . .

a. Kind of freak out; I don't like change.

b. Feel inspired.

c. Want to find myself in them.

d. Am receptive.

e. Want to meet everyone and learn everything.

f. Feel a little shy and reserved.

g. Thrive.

h. All of the above.

Your aura could be this color if you answered:

Mostly A—Red: *Grounded, passionate, materialism, business interactions, family oriented, strong*

....

Mostly B—Orange: *Creative, receptive, pregnant, ability to wake dreams into reality, needs being met*

....

Mostly C—Yellow: *Joy, health, new beginnings, positive thoughts, awareness, protected, addiction*

....

Mostly D—Green: *A natural healer, compassionate, empathy, love, parenting, very connected to the earth*

....

Mostly E—Blue: *Balance and deep need for balance to be maintained, organized, teacher, momentous life event on the horizon*

....

Mostly F—Indigo: *Game changer, difficult early life, here to help, strong sense of purpose, depression if not on path, sacred rebel*

....

Mostly G—Violet: *Dreamer, spiritually aware, shyness, protective, leader*

....

Mostly H or a mix of letters—Probably a dominant accent color like Silver, Gold, Magenta, or Opalescent

Acknowledgments

Photographer:
Ashley River Brant
ashleyriverbrant.love

Headshot Image:
Herman Hanekamp

Illustrator:
Cara Marie Piazza
caramariepiazza.com

Clothing:
Loup Charmant
Cara Marie Piazza
Matta NY

Hair:
Sondra Tillman

Crystals:
Dynamic Energy Crystals

Locations:
Home of True Botanicals
    founder Hillary
    Peterson

Writer, filmmaker, and
    founder of Nomad
    Studio

Tranquil, Artisan Studio
    & Garden, Mill Valley,
    CA

Tripp Carpenter, master
    studio furniture maker,
    Espenet Furniture,
    Bolinas, CA

Oceanview Retreat,
    Stinson Beach, CA,
    instagram.com/
    baytreebungalows

Redwood soaking
    tub: Andrew Brant,
    mtzionworkshop.com

William Morrow Team:
Liate Stehlik
Cassie Jones
Benjamin Steinberg
Emma Brodie
Shelby Peak
Bonni Leon-Berman
Yeon Kim
Mumtaz Mustafa
Susan Kosko
Molly Waxman
Alison Hinchcliffe

Thank You (Production):
Munay Hanekamp
Claire Michelle
Luciana Naclerio
Lindsay Bilezikian
Kelsea Kirsch
Annie Hwang
Steve Troha

Index

Drawings by Cara Piazza and Ashley Glynn
Photo on page 252 by Herman Hanekamp
All other photos by Ashley Glynn

HarperCollins books may be purchased for educational, business, or
sales promotional use. For information, please email the Special Markets
Department at SPsales@harpercollins.com.

FIRST EDITION

Designed by Bonni Leon-Berman

Library of Congress Cataloging-in-Publication Data has been applied for.

ISBN 978-0-06-291578-8

20 21 22 23 24   IM   10 9 8 7 6 5 4 3 2 1